Missouri Wildflowers

by

EDGAR DENISON

A Field Guide

to

Wildflowers of Missouri

and

Adjacent Areas

With 267 pictures in color and 435 described

Published by the

MISSOURI DEPARTMENT OF CONSERVATION
Post Office Box 180
Jefferson City, Missouri 65101

Third Revised Edition, 1978

DEDICATION

To my parents who instilled
the love of nature in me, and
to my wife who shares this
love with me.   *E.D.*

Preserve our Wildflowers
DO NOT PICK, DO NOT DIG!

This book has been donated by the author to the Missouri
Department of Conservation to further the cause of Nature
Appreciation and Conservation.

INTRODUCTION TO FIRST EDITION (DEC., 1972)

This book has been prepared to help the casual flower watcher as well as those more advanced in the delightful avocation of getting acquainted with our native wildflowers. It is an ambitious undertaking, with 250 flowers presented in color photographs and an additional 150 described. Botanists, the few professionals who can claim this title, do not need colored pictures for plant identification. They and a few advanced amateurs are able to use that magnificent work of Dr. Julian Steyermark, *Flora of Missouri*. Those of us who take our wildflower study more casually have been in need of help for a long time.

All plants shown and described in this book grow within the boundaries of Missouri. While the information on their habitat, distribution, and blooming time refers to Missouri only, these same plants can also be found in some or all adjacent states. Thus the book should be useful to many Midwestern flower lovers outside Missouri.

As a presentation of the Missouri Department of Conservation, the book fits into the Department's educational efforts to give more Missourians a better understanding of nature's wonders and delights. It is especially hoped that these pages will find their way into the hands of our young friends.

ACKNOWLEDGEMENTS

I am very grateful to Dr. Clair Kucera, professor of Biological Sciences of the University of Missouri at Columbia, for his help in preparation of the original manuscript. Mark Sullivan of the Missouri Department of Conservation deserves much credit for his many hours of editorial work in shaping this book, while James F. Keefe, Information Officer of the Conservation Department, encouraged and guided the planning.

Edgar Denison

INTRODUCTION TO THE THIRD EDITION (1978)

It is encouraging that in just four years, nearly 30,000 copies of *Missouri Wildflowers* have found their way to people who are ever more interested in Nature and Nature study.

The general format of this third edition remains unchanged, but within this frame a number of what is hoped to be improvements have been incorporated.

Ten species have been removed as they are believed to be too rare to be found by the average flower lover. Twenty-seven species of plants, commonly found, have been added in pictures and text, increasing the number of color pictures to 267. The text of plants described but not pictured has been enlarged and made uniform and the number of plants in this category has been increased to 168.

A new section has been added, providing a design for field identification of wildflowers through use of family characteristics. This section is illustrated by over 30 line drawings. A number of line drawings have been added to the text to facilitate identification.

A large number of pictures have been upgraded in the hope that this will be of help in the field.

We send this edition into the world asking all of you to remember and spread the gospel:

DO NOT PICK, DO NOT DIG WILDFLOWERS!

WILDFLOWER CONSERVATION

We have all seen a nosegay of wilted flowers thrown away along a field path, a sight encountered even in parks where picking flowers is specifically prohibited. A child—or a less innocent adult—was enchanted by the beauty of pretty flowers and picked them, only to see them wilt almost immediately. The idea that flowers are there for the picking is a mistaken one. It is one thing to "harvest" flowers which have been grown in gardens or nurseries and another when we deal with wildflowers.

Our expanding population and the ruthless demands of our technological civilization take enormous amounts of land, destroying all living things on it and endangering plant and animal species. Look at the huge number of houses and trailers which seem to mushroom in places which were forests and meadows only yesterday. And look at the devastation on our land through refuse dumps with discarded carcasses of cars, refrigerators, stoves, cans and bottles. Unguarded beauty spots, rich in flowers, become dumps overnight all over our state. Flowers disappear and we are poorer for it. Our negligent society has not yet found the strength to deal with this disease and it makes every wildflower that much more valuable.

Under these circumstances every plant must be protected from destruction. The flowers serve many purposes. They are there to procreate the species, they serve as food to many valuable insects, they also serve plant-eating animals, and after dying each fall they become life-giving humus.

Because sometimes, in some places, certain plants appear in great profusion we are tempted to look on them as expendable. This, again, is an error. Nature must not be disturbed willfully and cannot be disturbed without making our life poorer and duller. The wildflower lover will identify plants without picking them. Flowers are for all to enjoy—hopefully, for untold generations to come.

ABOUT THE BOOK AND HOW TO USE IT

Steyermark lists 2,369 flowering plants in Missouri. This includes the grasses, sedges, bur-weeds, pond-weeds, and duck-weeds, which have specialized flowering parts that are flowers to the botanist but hardly recognizeable as such to the amateur. Excluding these leaves us with 1,882 flowering plants.

Again, many of these plants have very tiny, insignificant flowers. Others are rarities—some have been reported only once or twice in Missouri many years ago. Still others are occasional escapees from flower and vegetable gardens. And individual members (species) of many plant groups (genera) are so much alike, or there are so many of them, that the casual flower lover will be satisfied if he can identify the genus. For example, there are in Missouri 50 species of Hawthorn, 29 kinds of Aster, 18 different Tickseed, just to name a few.

Thus, we believe that the plants pictured and described in this book represent a really worthwhile selection of the state's entire flora, particularly those plants with showy flowers.

For a further discussion of this subject refer to the chapter on "Plant Family Characteristics for Field Identification" on page 92.

Arrangement by Flower Colors

The flower pictures are arranged by colors to make identification as easy as possible. Three factors make such groupings difficult. First, flower colors are not usually a pure color, such as blue or red or yellow, but fall somewhere between these, such as purple or orange. Second, individual plant species often have a wide range of color variations. And finally, the color definition is highly subjective. Like beauty, it is in the eye of the beholder.

The selected groupings may seem arbitrary at times, but a choice had to be made. The color groups are: 1) white; 2) yellow, which includes cream and orange; 3) green, which includes greenish-white; 4) brown; 5) red, which includes pink and lavender; 6) blue, which includes purple and violet.

As an aid in locating the various color groups a color index tab has been printed on the margin of the picture pages. The greatest problems with color fall in the lavender-purple-violet range, so cross checking will be necessary if you are having trouble with identification. Lavender is included in the red group and purple and violet in the blue group.

Species With Color Variations

Many plants have one or more color variations. In general, many white flowers have pink variants and blue flowers may be found in white or purple specimens. Such color variations are mentioned in the text. When a flower is found which looks like one depicted but differs in color, consult the text.

Time of Blooming

Within each color group the plants are arranged in order of their earliest recorded blooming dates in Missouri. This sequence must, of necessity, be approximate. Many plants come into bloom at about the same time. Others have very long flowering seasons—some may be in bloom almost throughout the year. Still others with a distribution throughout the latitudes of Missouri come into bloom weeks earlier near the southern border than they do in the north. The blooming season for each species is given in the legend beside the picture.

Habitat

The "habitat" (from Latin *habitare,* "to dwell") of a plant is the environment in which it either prefers or demands to live. Sometimes the habitat requirements are very precise for soil, temperature range, moisture, light or shade, competition of other plants, tolerance to summer droughts or winter winds, or other factors. Sometimes plants will tolerate an amazing range of conditions and thus can be found in many places. The habitat description for tolerant plants can only be generalized.

Distribution

The distribution of a species is hardly ever a clearly defined one. Plants may appear and disappear in specific localities. Species distributions in this book are in part based on herbarium records, in part on field experience and in large part on reasonable expectations. Even with a liberal approach, it is quite likely that some species may at times be recorded in localities outside their shown range.

Common Names

Most wildflower lovers insist on using the common names of plants. This is unfortunate because it causes no end of confusion. The early travelers and settlers, seeing all kinds of flowers new to them, gave them names, often nostalgic reminders of posies of the "old country." Many of these names have disappeared, but others persisted locally, regionally, or even nationally. Some plants have a dozen, or even two dozen, different common names. (See *Houstonia minima,* page 225.) Others, botanically totally unrelated, have been given identical names. There is no authority, no law, no scientist who can accept or reject these common names.

Three plants from three different plant families are called Rattlesnake Master in Missouri. What a seedbed for arguments and misunderstandings! To avoid this problem the more serious student of plants has no choice but to learn and use botanical nomenclature.

Botanical Names

Every plant in this world can be precisely defined by two names. The first designates the genus (plural, genera), a group of closely related plants. The second tells the species—the individual, specific plants within the genus.

Botanical names are either Latin or Greek with Latin endings, and the naming method is called the binomial (Latin, "two-worded") system. As the botanical names are frequently descriptive, the text includes a translation, though authorities are not always in agreement as to the exact meaning of the translation. Many species names honor botanists or refer to American states *(pennsylvanicus, ohioensis, missouriensis)* in which the plants, shipped to Europe for classification, had been collected.

Genera are grouped into families and acquaintance with family characteristics is helpful in facilitating plant identification. Family names of plants in this book are included in the text as well as the common and botanical names.

Arrangement of Text

While the flower pictures are grouped by colors and within color in sequence of flowering time, the text is arranged by plant families. The sequence of families follows one used in almost all modern botanical references. First, the plants are separated between those with one seed-leaf, the monocotyledons, and the much larger group with two seed-leaves, the dicotyledons. Within these two groups the families are listed according to their evolutionary developments, beginning with the primitive and progressing to those considered most advanced.

Within the families the genera are presented in alphabetical order with the exception of the Composite family which has been arranged in 3 subsections, each giving the genera in alphabetical order.

THE METRIC SYSTEM

As our country moves slowly but surely toward acceptance of the metric system of measurements, it seemed desirable to include millimeters, centimeters and meters as well as inches and feet. As all measurements relating to living plants can only be approximate and do not have absolute value, the conversion, between the two systems was NOT based on scientifically or mathematically accurate equivalents but rather on reasonable approximations. One foot, therefore, was "translated" into 30 centimeters (cm), and ½ inch becomes 12 millimeters (mm). It would be ridiculous to work with millimeters when centimeters are close enough, and the same reasoning applies to meters as related to centimeters.

PHOTOGRAPHING WILDFLOWERS

The enjoyment of finding a beautiful or interesting flower is much enhanced if we can preserve this fleeting pleasure on film. A collection of wildflower pictures is not only esthetically rewarding but can be highly educational and helpful in the quest to learn plant names.

This is not the place for a technical treatise on flower photography, but a few thoughts may be of help. First, the nature photographer interested in wildflowers is not after salon pictures—those perfectly composed artistic creations which require either artificial arrangements and backgrounds or close-up views for other than botanical reasons.

What we want is a record of a plant, a record which must provide the essential features of the particular species by which identification can be accomplished. This is not always easily done. Consider a plant with basal leaves—a rosette of leaves at ground level—and a tall stalk on which flowers are borne. The Mullein and Prairie Dock are good examples. It is not possible to get a detailed picture of the entire plant with the universally favored 35 mm camera. We will have to make our record on two pictures, a general view of the plant and a closer view of the flowers.

Sharpness is necessary. The much-recommended tripod is a burden to be lugged around and is of no value at all to stop the ever-present wind. A fairly fast film IS desirable. The author uses ASA 64, but others prefer faster emulsions which permit fairly good pictures in shade. Portrait lens attachments are very good for closeup shots as are zoom lenses, the latter being a great deal more expensive. Advanced perfectionists may want to experiment with fill-in flash, but this technique is rarely required in the field.

A good light meter, either built into the camera or as separate equipment, is a requirement.

We must make a number of decisions about what we want to photograph. The intriguing vistas of massive wildflower displays are worthwhile subjects for background information, but are worthless as sources for plant identification. Try to select a healthy specimen. Leaves, as well as flowers, are essential. When a plant has leaves of varying shapes the picture must provide this information. Last, but not least, write down where you found the plant and on what date.

This is only the sketchiest of outlines. Books can be, and have been, written on the subject.

One last thought. Almost invariably when we want to take the picture of a wild flower or plant there are leaves or grasses or other plants in our way. We must clean up the view to get an acceptable picture. This should be done with the least destruction possible. Plants can be temporarily bent or tied away, but we have no right to pull up living plants just because we want to take a picture. Many of the prints in this book could have been clearer if destruction of their surroundings had been perpetrated. Such vandalism is not considered permissible.

Missouri Wildflowers

Color Plates

Erigenia bulbosa
Harbinger of Spring
January - April
Text page: 187

Saxifraga virginiensis
Early Saxifrage
February - June
Text page: 147

Claytonia virginica
Spring Beauty
February - May
Also pink.
Text page: 130

Anemonella thalictroides
Rue Anemone
March - June
Also pink.
Text page: 135

Hepatica nobilis
Liverleaf
March - April
Also pink, purple.
Text page: 137

Isopyrum biternatum
False Rue Anemone
March - May
Text page: 138

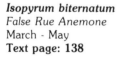

2

Erythronium albidum
Dog-tooth Violet
March - May
Yellow — *E. americanum, p. 119*
Text page: 118

Dentaria laciniata
Toothwort
March - May
Also pale lavender.
Text page: 145

Dicentra cucullaria
Dutchman's Breeches
March - May
Also pink.
Text page: 143

3

Podophyllum peltatum
May Apple
March - May
Text page: 140

Nothoscordum bivalve
False Garlic
March - May
Text page: 120

Amelanchier arborea
Shadbush
March - May
Text page: 148

Antennaria plantaginifolia
Pussy's Toes
April - June
Also off-white to pink.
Text page: 237

Cardamine bulbosa
Spring Cress
March - June
Text page: 144

Sanguinaria canadensis
Bloodroot
March - April
Text page: 142

5

Lepidium campestre
Pepper Grass
April - June
Text page: 145

Prunus americana
Wild Plum
April - May
Text page: 154

Prunus serotina
Black Cherry
April - May
Text page: 154

Trillium flexipes
White Trillium
April - May
Text page: 121

Clematis fremontii
Fremont's Leather Flower
April - May
Also dull lavender.
Text page: 136

Ribes missouriense
Wild Gooseberry
April - May
Also greenish.
Text page: 147

Erigeron philadelphicus
Philadelphia Fleabane
April - June
Also light pink.
Text page: 255

Anemone virginiana
Thimbleweed
April - August
Text page: 135

Nasturtium officinale
Water Cress
April - October
Also pale lavender.
Text page: 146

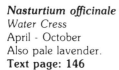

8

Cornus florida
Flowering Dogwood
April - May
Rarely pink.
Text page: 190

Viburnum rufidulum
Southern Black Haw
April - May
Text page: 228

Staphylea trifolia
American Bladder-nut
April - May
Text page: 173

9

Camassia scilloides
Wild Hyacinth
April - May
Also with bluish tint.
Text page: 118

Osmorhiza claytoni
Sweet Cicely
April - June
Text page: 188

Houstonia longifolia
Long-leaved Houstonia
April - July
Text page: 226

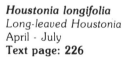

Rubus flagellaris
Dewberry
April - June
Text page: 156

Crataegus
Hawthorn
April - May
Text page: 151

Fragaria virginiana
Wild Strawberry
April - May
Text page: 152

11

Plantago lanceolata
English Plantain
April - October
Text page: 224

Ornithogalum umbellatum
Star of Bethlehem
April - May
Text page: 120

Hydrastis canadensis
Golden Seal
April - May
Text page: 137

Vaccinium vacillans
Lowbush Blueberry
April - May
Also greenish.
Text page: 192

Vaccinium stamineum
Highbush Huckleberry
April - June
Text page: 192

Ptelea trifoliata
Hop Tree
April - June
Text page: 167

Smilacina racemosa
False Solomon's Seal
May - June
Text page: 121

Torilis japonica
Hedge Parsley
June - August
Text page: 189

Anemone canadensis
White Anemone
May - July
Text page: 134

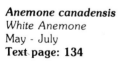

14

Viburnum rafinesquianum
Arrow-wood
May - June
Text page: 229

Verbascum blattaria
Moth Mullein
May - September
Also yellow.
Text page: 221

Polygonatum
    commutatum
Solomon's Seal
May - June
Text page: 120

15

Physocarpus opulifolius
Ninebark
May - June
Text page: 153

Ceanothus americanus
New Jersey Tea
May
Text page: 175

Sambucus canadensis
Elderberry
May - July
Text page: 227

16

Lobelia spicata
Spiked Lobelia
May - August
Also light blue.
Text page: 230

Aruncus dioicus
Goat's Beard
May - July
Text page: 151

Convolvulus sepium
Hedge Bindweed
May - September
Also pink.
Text page: 200

17

Parthenium integrifolium
American Feverfew
May - September
Text page: 261

Datura stramonium
Jimson Weed
May - October
Also pale violet.
Text page: 214

Ipomoea pandurata
Wild Potato Vine
May - September
Also light purple or rose.
Text page: 200

18

Geum canadense
White Avens
May - October
Also light pink.
Text page: 152

Gillenia stipulata
Indian Physic
May - July
Text page: 152

Robinia pseudo-acacia
Black Locust
May - June
Text page: 164

19

Penstemon digitalis
Beard-tongue
May - July
Text page: 220

Verbena simplex
Narrow-leaved Verbena
May - September
Also light violet.
Text page: 208

Cornus obliqua
Swamp Dogwood
May - July
Text page: 190

Daucus carota
Queen Anne's Lace
May - October
Also pinkish.
Text page: 187

Baptisia leucantha
White Wild Indigo
May - July
Blue or violet — B. australis, p. 158.
Text page: 157

Hydrangea arborescens
Wild Hydrangea
May - July
Text page: 146

21

Achillea millefolium
Yarrow
May - November
Also pink.
Text page: 249

Chrysanthemum leucanthemum
Ox-eye Daisy
May - August
Text page: 251

Lippia lanceolata
Fog Fruit
May - September
Also light pink.
Text page: 207

Apocynum cannabinum
Dogbane
May - August
Text page: 195

Yucca smalliana
Spanish Bayonet
May - August
Text page: 122

Euphorbia corollata
Flowering Spurge
May - October
Text page: 168

Silene stellata
Starry Campion
June - September
Text page: 132

Veronicastrum virginicum
Culver's-root
June - September
Text page: 222

Polymnia canadensis
Leaf-cup
May - October
Text page: 261

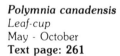

Cacalia atriplicifolia
Pale Indian Plantain
June - September
Text page: 238

Gaura biennis
Gaura
June - October
Pink when fading.
Text page: 185

Cephalanthus occidentalis
Buttonbush
June - September
Text page: 225

Pycnanthemum tenuifolium
Slender Mountain Mint
June - September
Also light lavender.
Text page: 212

Eupatorium rugosum
White Snakeroot
July - October
Text page: 241

Polygonum scandens
Climbing False Buckwheat
July - November
Text page: 128

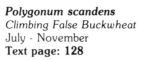

26

Verbesina virginica
White Crown-beard
August - October
Text page: 270

Aster pilosus
White Heath Aster
August - November
Also purplish.
Text page: 250

Cynanchum laeve
Angle-pod
July - September
Text page: 199

Spiranthes cernua
Ladies' Tresses
August - November
Text page: 126

Eupatorium altissimum
Tall Thoroughwort
August - October
Text page: 241

Elephantopus carolinianus
Elephant's Foot
August - October
Also light lavender.
Text page: 240

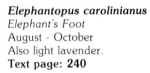

Ranunculus harveyi
Harvey's Buttercup
March - May
Text page: 138

Ranunculus hispidus
Hispid Buttercup
March - June
Text page: 138

Lithospermum canescens
Hoary Puccoon
March - June
Text page: 206

29

Lindera benzoin
Spice bush
March - May
Text page: 141

Sassafras albidum
Sassafras
April - May
Text page: 141

Viola pensylvanica
Smooth Yellow Violet
March - May
Text page: 183

Hypoxis hirsuta
Yellow Star Grass
April - May
Text page: 123

Pedicularis canadensis
Lousewort
April - May
Text page: 219

Astragalus mexicanus
Ground Plum
March - May
Text page: 157

31

Corydalis flavula
Pale Corydalis
April - May
Text page: 142

Uvularia grandiflora
Bellwort
April - May
Text page: 122

Lonicera flava
Yellow Honeysuckle
April - May
Text page: 226

32

Brassica nigra
Black Mustard
April - November
Text page: 144

Barbarea vulgaris
Yellow Rocket
April - June
Text page: 143

Stylophorum diphyllum
Celandine Poppy
April - June
Text page: 142

33

Cypripedium calceolus
Yellow Lady-slipper
April - June
Text page: 125

Senecio obovatus
Squaw-weed
April - June
Text page: 265

Baptisia leucophaea
Long-bracted Wild Indigo
April - June
Text page: 157

Coreopsis lanceolata
Tickseed Coreopsis
April - July
Also greenish-white.
Text page: 251

Aesculus glabra
Ohio Buckeye
April - May
Text page: 174

Potentilla simplex
Cinquefoil
April - June
Text page: 153

Erysimum capitatum
Western Wall-flower
May - July
Text page: 145

Melilotus officinalis
Yellow Sweet Clover
May - October
White — *M. albus*, p. 162
Text page: 162

Oxalis stricta
Yellow Wood Sorrel
May - October
Text page: 166

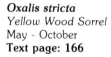

Tragopon dubius
Goat's Beard
May - July
Purple — *T. porrifolius, p. 237*
Text page: 237

Pastinaca sativa
Parsnip
May - October
Text page: 188

Oenothera missouriensis
Missouri Evening Primrose
May - August
Text page: 186

37

Pyrrhopappus carolinianus
False Dandelion
May - October
Text page: 234

Krigia biflora
Dwarf Dandelion
May - August
Text page: 233

Opuntia compressa
Prickly Pear
May - July
Text page: 184

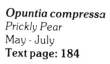

Lysimachia lanceolata
Loosestrife
May - August
Text page: 193

Hemerocallis fulva
Day Lily
May - August
Text page: 119

Thaspium trifoliatum
Meadow Parsnip
April - June
Rarely purple, brownish-
    purple
Text page: 189

39

Potentilla recta
Rough-fruited Cinquefoil
May - August
Text page: 154

Solanum rostratum
Buffalo Bur
May - October
Text page: 215

Asclepias tuberosa
Butterfly-weed
May - September
Rarely yellow.
Text page: 197

Hieracium gronovii
Hawkweed
May - October
Text page: 232

Physalis longifolia
Ground Cherry
May - September
Text page: 214

Impatiens capensis
Spotted Touch-me-not
May - October
Yellow — *I. pallida, p. 175*
Text page: 175

41

Stylosanthes biflora
Pencil Flower
May - September
Text page: 165

Hypericum perforatum
Common St. John's-wort
May - September
Text page: 177

Rudbeckia hirta
Black-eyed Susan
May - October
Text page: 262

Verbascum thapsus
Mullein
May - September
Text page: 221

Verbesina helianthoides
Wing-stem
May - October
Text page: 270

Lotus corniculatus
Bird's-foot Trefoil
May - October
Text page: 162

Lilium michiganense
Turk's Cap Lily
June - July
Text page: 119

Ratibida pinnata
Gray-head Coneflower
May - September
Text page: 262

Rudbeckia triloba
Brown-eyed Susan
June - November
Text page: 265

44

Ludwigia alternifolia
False Loosestrife
June - August
Text page: 185

Oenothera biennis
Evening Primrose
June - September
Text page: 185

Hypericum spathulatum
Shrubby St. John's-wort
June - September
Text page: 178

45

Nelumbo lutea
American Lotus
June - September
Text page: 133

Cassia fasciculata
Partridge Pea
June - October
Text page: 158

Helenium amarum
Sneezeweed
June - November
Text page: 256

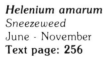

Coreopsis tripteris
Tall Tickseed
July - September
Text page: 252

Solidago juncea
Early Goldenrod
June - October
Text page: 269

Chrysopsis villosa
Golden Aster
June - October
Text page: 251

47

Silphium perfoliatum
Cup Plant
July - September
Text page: 266

Silphium terebinthinaceum
Prairie Dock
July - October
Text page: 269

Sida spinosa
Prickly Sida
June - October
Text page: 176

Helianthus grosseserratus
Sawtooth Sunflower
July - October
Text page: 258

Helianthus tuberosus
Jerusalem Artichoke
August - October
Text page: 257

Ascyrum hypericoides
St. Andrew's Cross
July - October
Text page: 177

49

Cassia marilandica
Wild Senna
July - August
Text page: 158

Belamcanda chinensis
Blackberry Lily
July - August
Text page: 124

Solidago speciosa
Goldenrod
August - November
Text page: 270

Bidens polylepis
Beggar-ticks
August - October
Text page: 250

Helenium autumnale
Sneezeweed
August - November
Text page: 257

Gerardia pedicularia
Fern-leaved False Foxglove
August - September
Text page: 219

Hybanthus concolor
Green Violet
April - June
Text page: 179

Euphorbia commutata
Wood Spurge
April - July
Text page: 168

Rumex altissimus
Pale Dock
April - May
Text page: 129

Arisaema dracontium
Green Dragon
April - June
Text page: 115

Swertia caroliniensis
American Columbo
May - June
Text page: 195

Phytolacca americana
Pokeweed
May - October
Text page: 130

53

Vitis vulpina
Winter Grape
May - June
Text page: 176

Rhus glabra
Smooth Sumac
May - July
Text page: 170

Rhus radicans
Poison Ivy
May - July
Also nearly white.
Text page: 173

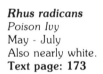

54

Thalictrum revolutum
Waxy Meadow Rue
May - July
Also light purple.
Text page: 140

Agave virginica
American Aloe
June - August
Text page: 123

Eryngium yuccifolium
Yucca-leaf Eryngo
July - August
Text page: 188

55

Ambrosia trifida
Ragweed
July - September
Text page: 271

Asimina triloba
Pawpaw
March - May
Text page: 134

Arisaema atrorubens
Jack-in-the-Pulpit
April - June
Also all green.
Text page: 115

Asarum canadense
Wild Ginger
April - May
Text page: 126

Trillium sessile
Wake Robin
April - June
Variable color.
Text page: 121

I_F You Want Wildflowers
In Your Garden
Grow Them From Seeds
Do Not Dig Them !

Matelea decipiens
Climbing Milkweed
May - June
Text page: 199

Triosteum perfoliatum
Common Horse Gentian
May - July
Text page: 228

Scrophularia marilandica
Figwort
July - October
Text page: 221

Cercis canadensis
Redbud
March - May
Text page: 159

Verbena canadensis
Rose Verbena
March - November
Text page: 207

Lamium amplexicaule
Henbit
February - November
Text page: 210

Hydrophyllum appendiculatum
Woolen Breeches
April - July
Text page: 202

Lamium purpureum
Dead Nettle
April - October
Also rarely white.
Text page: 210

Acer rubrum
Red Maple
March - April
Also orange.
Text page: 174

Castilleja coccinea
Indian Paint-brush
April - July
Also yellow.
Text page: 216

Geranium maculatum
Wild Geranium
April - June
Text page: 167

Dodecatheon meadia
Shooting Star
April - June
Also white.
Text page: 193

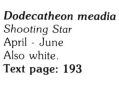

62

Monarda russeliana
Horsemint
April - June
Also lavender, whitish.
Text page: 211

Pyrus ioensis
Wild Crab
April - May
Also white.
Text page: 155

Rhododendron roseum
Azalea
April - May
Also white.
Text page: 191

Aquilegia canadensis
Columbine
April - July
Text page: 135

Oxalis violacea
Violet Wood Sorrel
April - July
Rarely white.
Text page: 166

Silene virginica
Fire Pink
April - June
Text page: 132

64

Asclepias quadrifolia
Four-leaved Milkweed
May - July
Also white.
Text page: 197

Lathyrus latifolius
Everlasting Pea
May - September
Also white.
Text page: 160

Tephrosia virginiana
Goat's Rue
May - August
Text page: 165

65

Mirabilis nyctaginea
Wild Four-o'clock
May - October
Text page: 129

Echinacea pallida
Pale-purple Coneflower
May - July
Rarely white.
Text page: 252

Rosa setigera
Prairie Rose
May - July
Rarely white.
Text page: 155

Asclepias syriaca
Common Milkweed
May - August
Text page: 198

Asclepias purpurascens
Purple Milkweed
May - July
Text page: 197

Campsis radicans
Trumpet Creeper
May - August
Text page: 222

Talinum calycinum
Rock Pink
May - August
Text page: 131

Lespedeza virginica
Bush Clover
May - September
Text page: 161

Oenothera speciosa
Showy Evening Primrose
May - July
Also white.
Text page: 186

Vernonia baldwini
Ironweed
May - September
Text page: 246

Dianthus armeria
Deptford Pink
May - October
Text page: 131

Coronilla varia
Crown Vetch
May - August
Also white.
Text page: 159

Physostegia virginiana
False Dragonhead
May - September
Text page: 211

Blephilia ciliata
Ohio Horsemint
May - August
Text page: 209

Ruellia strepens
Wild Petunia
May - October
Rarely white.
Text page: 223

Schrankia uncinata
Sensitive Brier
May - September
Text page: 164

Anagallis arvensis
Pimpernel
May - September
Rarely white.
Text page: 193

Clitoria mariana
Butterfly Pea
May - September
Text page: 159

Sabatia angularis
Rose Gentian
June - September
Also white.
Text page: 194

Lythrum alatum
Winged Loosestrife
June - September
Text page: 184

Dipsacus sylvestris
Teasel
June - October
Text page: 229

Cirsium vulgare
Bull Thistle
June - September
Text page: 240

Carduus nutans
Musk Thistle
June - October
Text page: 239

Petalostemon purpureum
Purple Prairie Clover
June - September
White — *P. candidum, p. 163*
Text page: 162

73

Saponaria officinalis
Soapwort
June - October
Also white.
Text page: 133

Teucrium canadense
Wood Sage
June - September
Text page: 213

Polygonum coccineum
Water Smartweed
June - October
Text page: 127

74

Hibiscus lasiocarpos
Rose Mallow
July - October
Also white.
Text page: 176

Lobelia cardinalis
Cardinal Flower
July - October
White very rare.
Text page: 231

Allium stellatum
Wild Onion
July - November
Also white.
Text page: 117

Cunila origanoides
Dittany
July - November
Text page: 210

Lespedeza violacea
Bush Clover
July - September
Text page: 161

Phlox paniculata
Perennial Phlox
July - October
Also purple, white.
Text page: 201

Liatris aspera
Blazing Star
August - November
Rarely white.
Text page: 242

Liatris pycnostachia
Blazing Star
July - October
Rarely white.
Text pages: 245

Desmodium canescens
Tick-trefoil
July - September
Text page: 160

77

Aster novae-angliae
New England Aster
August - October
Variable colors.
Text page: 249

Gerardia tenuifolia
Gerardia
August - October
Rarely white.
Text page: 216

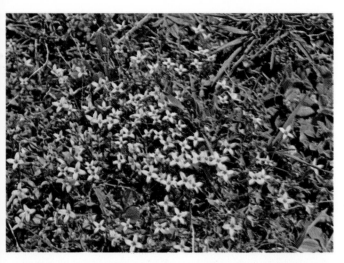

Houstonia minima
Least Bluets
January - April
Also white.
Text page: 225

Viola rafinesquii
Johnny-jump-up
March - May
Also nearly white.
Text page: 183

Viola sororia
Woolly Blue Violet
March - June
Text page: 180

79

Phlox bifida
Sand Phlox
March - May
Rarely white.
Text page: 201

Mertensia virginica
Bluebells
March - June
Also pink, white.
Text page: 207

Phlox divaricata
Wild Sweet William
April - June
Variable colors, rarely white.
Text page: 201

Sisyrinchium campestre
Prairie Blue-eyed Grass
April - June
Also white or yellow.
Text page: 125

Delphinium tricorne
Dwarf Larkspur
April - June
Also purple or white.
Text page: 136

Polemonium reptans
Jacob's Ladder
April - June
Text page: 202

81

Vicia villosa
Hairy Vetch
April - October
Text page: 165

Specularia perfoliata
Venus' Looking Glass
April - August
Rarely white.
Text page: 231

Collinsia verna
Blue-eyed Mary
April - June
Also lavender, white.
Text page: 216

Tradescantia longipes
Wild Crocus
April - May
Variable colors.
Text page: 117

Viola pedata lineariloba
Bird's-foot Violet
April - June
Also lavender, white.
Text page: 179

Viola pedata pedata
Bird's-foot Violet
April - June
Text page: 179

Nemastylis geminiflora
Celestial Lily
April - May
Text page: 124

Cynoglossum virginianum
Wild Comfrey
April - June
Also whitish.
Text page: 205

Phacelia purshii
Miami Mist
April - June
Also whitish.
Text page: 205

Delphinium carolinianum
Carolina Larkspur
May - June
Also violet or white.
Text page: 136

Iris virginica
Southern Blue Flag
May - July
Also white to deep violet.
Text page: 124

Amsonia illustris
Blue Star
April - May
Text page: 195

85

Tradescantia ohiensis
Spiderwort
May - July
Variable, rarely white.
Text page: 116

Amorpha canescens
Lead Plant
May - August
Text page: 156

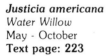

Justicia americana
Water Willow
May - October
Text page: 223

86

Prunella vulgaris
Heal-all
May - September
Rarely white.
Text page: 212

Echium vulgare
Viper's Bugloss
May - September
Variable colors.
Text page: 206

Centaurea cyanus
Cornflower
May - September
Also pink, whitish.
Text page: 239

Psoralea onobrychis
French Grass
May - September
Text page: 163

Commelina communis
Day-flower
May - October
Text page: 116

Cichorium intybus
Chicory
May - October
Rarely white.
Text page: 232

Verbena hastata
Blue Vervain
June - October
Variable, including white.
Text page: 208

Campanula americana
Tall Bellflower
June - October
Rarely white.
Text page: 230

Scutellaria incana
Skullcap
June - September
Text page: 213

89

Lactuca floridana
False Lettuce
August - October
Also nearly white.
Text page: 233

Lobelia siphilitica
Blue Lobelia
August - October
Also purple, white.
Text page: 231

Eupatorium coelestinum
Mist Flower
July - October
Text page: 242

90

Gentiana andrewsii
Closed Gentian
August - October
Variable colors.
Text page: 194

Aster turbinellus
Prairie Aster
August - November
Also lavender.
Text page: 250

PLANT FAMILY CHARACTERISTICS FOR FIELD IDENTIFICATION

92

Basic Botanical Terms

The appearance of plants, their leaves, flowers, floral arrangement, flowering season and habitat give the clues by which we try to identify them.

LEAVES are either simple or compound. They vary in shape and their leaf margins. They are either pinnately veined (like a feather) or parallel veined. Pinnately veined leaves are associated with the larger group of the angiosperms—those plants which produce their fruit in an ovary—which have two seed leaves, while those with one seed leaf produce parallel veined leaves.

FLOWERS are either regular or irregular. A "regular" flower cut along any axis, will present like sections. The "irregular" flower can be cut usually only along one axis to show like sections, or it may be totally asymmetrical. Bilateral symmetry is another expression for an irregular flower.

Flowers may have individual sepals and petals or may be in a tubular shape with lobes indicating the petals and sepals. Tubular flowers can be either regular or irregular.

Position of OVARY. In some cases it is helpful to know if the petals, sepals and stamens are inserted in the floral structure above or below the organ from which fruits develop. Depending on that arrangement, the ovary is either superior or inferior.

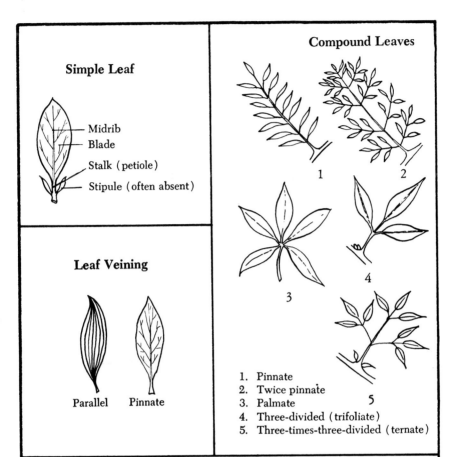

Simple Leaf

— Midrib
— Blade
— Stalk (petiole)
— Stipule (often absent)

Leaf Veining

Parallel   Pinnate

Compound Leaves

1
2
3
4
5

1. Pinnate
2. Twice pinnate
3. Palmate
4. Three-divided (trifoliate)
5. Three-times-three-divided (ternate)

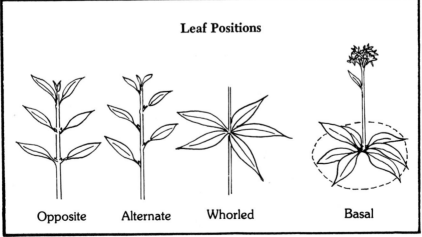

Leaf Positions

Opposite   Alternate   Whorled   Basal

Leaf Shapes

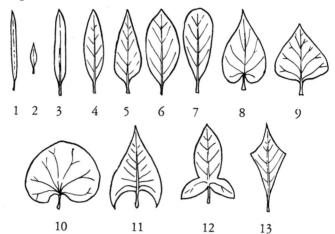

1. Needle-shaped (acicular)
2. Awl-shaped (subulate)
3. Linear
4. Oblong
5. Lance-shaped (lanceolate)
6. Ovate
7. Spoon-shaped (spatulate)
8. Heart-shaped (cordate)
9. Triangular (deltoid)
10. Kidney-shaped (reniform)
11. Arrow-shaped (sagittate)
12. Halberd-shaped (hastate)
13. Wedge-shaped (cuneate)

Leaf Margins

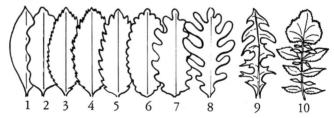

1. Entire
2. Wavy (undulate)
3. Toothed (serrate)
4. Double toothed (double serrate)
5. Coarsely toothed (dentate)
6. Rounded toothed (crenate)
7. Lobed
8. Parted
9. Incised
10. Pinnately (like a feather) divided
11. Palmately (like a hand) divided

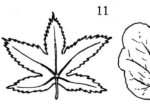

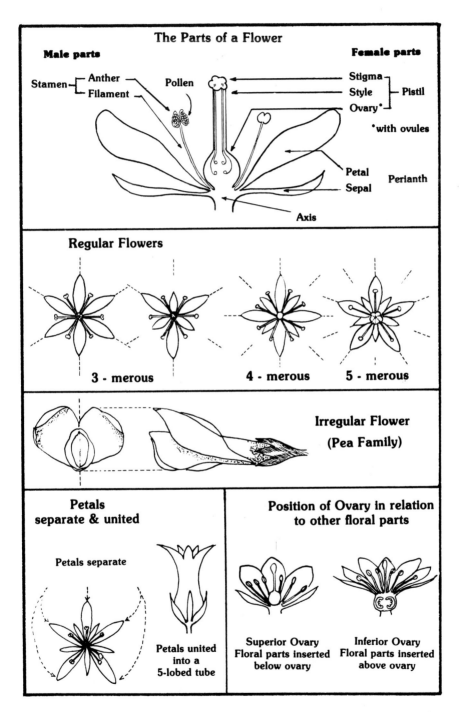

The Parts of a Flower

Male parts　　　　　　　　　　　　　　　　**Female parts**

Stamen ⌈ Anther　　Pollen　　　　　Stigma ⌉
　　　 ⌊ Filament　　　　　　　　　Style　⌉ Pistil
　　　　　　　　　　　　　　　　　Ovary*⌋

*with ovules

Petal　　Perianth
Sepal

Axis

Regular Flowers

3 - merous　　　　**4 - merous**　　　　**5 - merous**

Irregular Flower
(Pea Family)

Petals
separate & united

Petals separate

Petals united
into a
5-lobed tube

Position of Ovary in relation
to other floral parts

Superior Ovary
Floral parts inserted
below ovary

Inferior Ovary
Floral parts inserted
above ovary

ARRANGEMENTS OF INFLORESCENCES

Peduncle: A stalk to a solitary flower or an inflorescence

Pedicel : A stalk to a single flower of an inflorescence

TERMINAL FLOWER The inflorescence is carried at the tip of the stem(s).

AXILLARY FLOWER Flowers, either with or without pedicels, arise from leaf-joints. Stipules may or may not be present.

SPIKE Flowers without pedicels emerge from a more or less elongated axis. Flowering begins at the bottom.

RACEME Flowers on pedicels, which arise from a more or less elongated axis, the peduncle. Younger flowers toward the tip.

CORYMB A flat-topped or convex, open inflorescence. The pedicels of varying length. If the inflorescence consists of only one peduncle, it is a "simple corymb," if several peduncles combine to form the inflorescence, it becomes a "compound corymb."

CYME A flower cluster in which the central or terminal flower opens first.

UMBEL A flat-topped or convex inflorescence, consisting of many small flowers, each on a pedicel. The pedicels arise from one point.

If the inflorescence has only one point from which the pedicels arise, it is a "simple umbel". If a number of small umbels (called umbellets) are connected by stalks (called rays) to a central focal point, the umbel is compound. In the Family Apiaceae (formerly Umbelliferae) the Umbel form of inflorescence is characteristic.

The focal points of both pedicels and rays are subtended by a set of bracts (involucre of bracts).

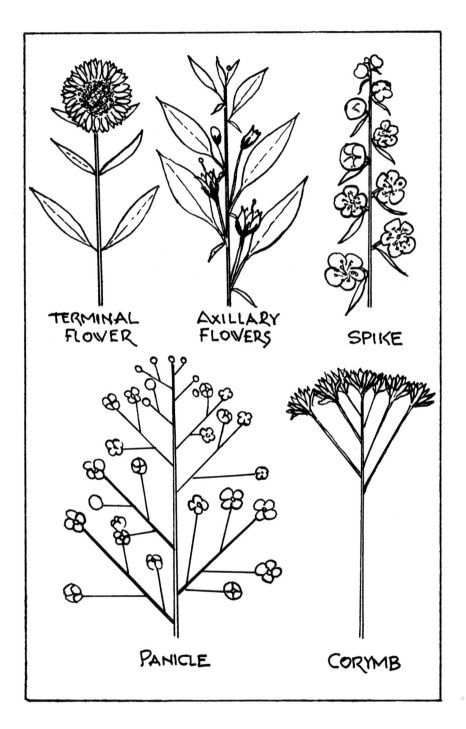

TERMINAL
FLOWER

AXILLARY
FLOWERS

SPIKE

97

PANICLE

CORYMB

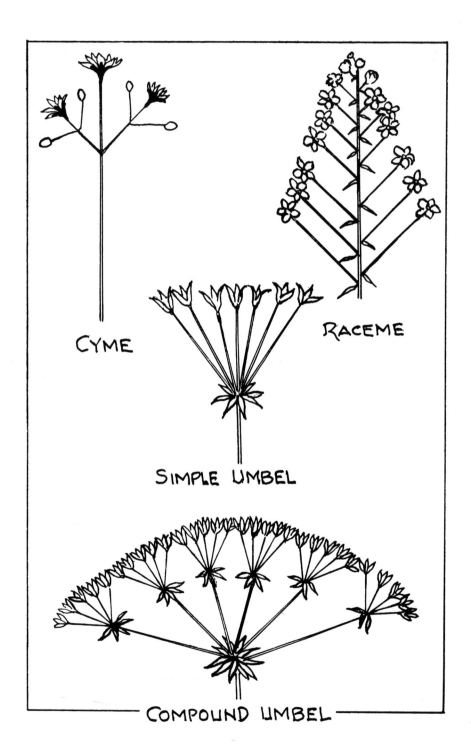

CYME

RACEME

SIMPLE UMBEL

COMPOUND UMBEL

98

PLANT FAMILY CHARACTERISTICS FOR
FIELD IDENTIFICATION

Steyermark, in his monumental *Flora of Missouri,* lists 2,372 species of Angiosperms—plants which form their fruit in an ovary—that have been reported found in Missouri. For our purposes of field identification, we can reduce this total substantially by eliminating:

    1. Grasses and Sedges—specialized flowering plants, and the Duckweeds and Rushes ....485 species.

    2. Railroad-yard adventives, which have not survived or were eliminated by weed-killers ....100 species.

    3. Garden and agricultural plants, which escaped from cultivation and usually cannot survive on their own ....125 species.

    4. Trees ....110 species.

    5. Rare plants, found between 50 and 100 years ago in one or two localities, whose existence in Missouri is doubtful or has terminated .... 70 species.

Thus, we can eliminate 890 species. This reduction leaves us with 1,482 species in 111 Families.

Plant Families

Amateur botanists expect family descriptions to be a matter of clear and crisp definitions with sharp boundaries between families. This, unfortunately, is not the case. An authority on taxonomy, George H. T. Lawrence, writes that "the family . . . is composed of one or more genera whose similarities are greater than their differences"—not an encouraging statement. Some families lend themselves to rather simple descriptions, but others are mixtures of many features which must be fitted together like pieces of a puzzle.

It is obvious that nobody would memorize all the features of the 111 families with which we deal. But, even if this computer-like feat were accomplished, it would be of little value for field identification, because so many characteristics can only be found through dissection and the use of the microscope. While destruction and collecting of plants may be justifiable in rare cases for botanical research, it cannot be condoned for amateurs and, especially, teachers in all levels of education who wrongly equate collecting with some degree of knowledge. Our reservoir of wildflowers is constantly shrinking. It is a widespread requirement that students of wildflowers should know the family connection of a plant. This makes sense only if the family name is tied to a meaningful concept of the primary botanical features of a given family. When this knowledge has been acquired, it can be a real help in field identification.

Luckily, we find on further study that 79% of the Missouri plant species are distributed in only 24 families. These are:

	Family	species
1. Asteraceae (Compositae)	Composites	274
2. Fabaceae (Leguminosae)	Pea	114
3. Rosaceae	Rose	93
4. Lamiaceae (Labiatae)	Mint	60
5. Brassicaceae (Cruciferae)	Mustard	59
6. Scrophulariaceae	Figwort	57
7. Ranunculaceae	Crowfoot	48
8. Apiaceae (Umbelliferae)	Carrot	43
9. Liliaceae	Lily	41
10. Caryophyllaceae	Pink	39
11. Polygonaceae	Buckwheat	39
12. Euphorbiaceae	Spurge	36
13. Orchidaceae	Orchid	31
14. Onagraceae	Evening Primrose	29
15. Chenopodiaceae	Goosefoot	27
16. Rubiaceae	Bedstraw	24
17. Boraginaceae	Forget-me-not	23
18. Solanaceae	Nightshade	21
19. Convolvulaceae	Morning Glory	20
20. Malvaceae	Mallow	20
21. Asclepiadaceae	Milkweed	20
22. Caprifoliaceae	Honeysuckle	19
23. Saxifragaceae	Saxifrage	17
24. Violaceae	Violet	15
		1,169

100

The distribution of three-quarters of the Missouri wildflower species in relatively few families gives us an important tool for field identification. If we acquaint ourselves with certain readily (and not so readily) visible characteristics of the large families, we have cleared the most difficult hurdle. Once we have determined the family to which a species belongs, the task of giving that plant its proper name is made easier with the help of a field-guide or wildflower book. On the following pages is a tabulation of family "marks" which with patience and practice can be stored in our memory.

Three families, listed above, are excluded from the tabulation for these reasons: the *Chenopodiaceae*—the Goosefoot or Pigweed Family —consists of weedy plants of little interest to an amateur flower-lover; the *Caprifoliaceae* are represented in our state primarily by two genera, the Viburnums—all of them shrubs—and the Honeysuckles—mostly climbers—which can be recognized readily without reference to family traits; last, the *Saxifragaceae* have so many rare members that not too many will be found without searching. In their stead, three other families have been inserted: *Iridaceae, Ericaceae* and *Commelinaceae*.

Twenty-four Plant Families, arranged according to basic floral appearance

A. MONOCOTYLEDONS
   3-merous
      Liliaceae (Lily)
      Iridaceae (Iris)
      Commelinaceae (Spiderwort)
      Orchidaceae (Orchid)

B. DICOTYLEDONS
   4 petals or lobes—regular flowers
      Brassicaceae (Mustard)
      Onagraceae (Evening Primrose)
      Rubiaceae (Madder)

   5 petals or lobes—regular flowers
      Malvaceae (Mallow)   ⎫
      Rosaceae (Rose)   ⎪
      Caryophyllaceae (Pink)   ⎬ petals
      Polygonaceae (Smartweed)[1] ⎪
      Apiaceae (in umbels) (Parsnip) ⎭
      Solanceae (Nightshade) ⎫ lobes
      Boraginaceae (Borage) ⎭

   5 petals or lobes—irregular flowers
      Scrophulariaceae (Figwort)[2]   ⎫
      Lamiaceae (Mint) 2 lips   ⎬ lobes
      Ericaceae (Heath)   ⎪
      Convolvulaceae (Morning Glory)[3] ⎭
      Fabaceae (Pea)   ⎫ petals
      Violaceae (Violet) ⎭

   Special floral arrangements
      Asclepiadaceae (Milkweed) 5-merous
      Asteraceae (Composite) flower-heads
      Euphorbiaceae (Spurge)
      Ranunculaceae (Buttercup)[4]

[1]Petaloid—no petals; the sepals act as petals.
[2]Genus Scrophularia has only 3 lips.
[3]Lobes often indistinct.
[4]Those species which have petals or petaloid sepals may have 5 or more.

It is most important to realize that the following is NOT a complete listing of all the features which collectively determine a family, but rather a selective description of pertinent "ear-marks" which can be used in the field.

PLANT FAMILY CHARACTERISTICS

FAMILY	PETALS OR LOBES	SEPALS	STAMENS	OVARY, PISTIL
MONOCOTYLEDON FAMILIES — parallel-veined leaves, flowers 3-merous				
Liliaceae Lily Figure 1, p. 110	3 petals	3 — often look like petals	6	ovary superior
Iridaceae Iris Figure 2, p. 110	3 petals	3	3	ovary inferior
Commelinaceae Spiderwort Figure 3, p. 110	3 petals often rounded	3 green	6 (Note 1)	ovary superior
Orchidaceae Orchid Figure 4, p. 110	3 petals sometimes difficult to recognize (Note 3)	3 sometimes 2 are joined or "fused"	1 or 2 attached to style (Note 3)	ovary inferior
DICOTYLEDON FAMILIES — arranged according to basic floral appearance				
REGULAR FLOWERS WITH 4 PETALS OR LOBES				
Brassicaceae (formerly *Cruciferae*) Mustard Figure 5, p. 110	4 petals in cross position	4 green	6 (Note 4)	ovary superior
Onagraceae Evening Primrose Figure 6, p. 111	4 petals sometimes connected to a long tube (Note 5)	4 often united to form a long tube	4~8 (Note 5)	ovary inferior stigma 4-lobed, cross-shaped
Rubiaceae Madder Figure 7, p. 111	4-lobed corolla tube	4-lobed united	4 alternate with lobes	ovary inferior

FOR FIELD IDENTIFICATION

LEAVES	OTHER CHARACTERISTICS, REMARKS AND NOTES	
mostly narrow, but wide in Trillium	Petals and sepals often look alike.	103
narrow and long	The erect petals are the "standards;" the decurved sepals are called "falls."	
form sheath around stem (Note 2)	1: Sometimes only 2 or 3 are fertile. The filaments often are hairy and highly colored. Flowers appear triangular in terminal clusters. They open in the morning only. Petals equal-sized in *Tradescantia,* while lower petal in *Commelina* is smaller. Color range: blue, purple, magenta. 2: Swollen nodes at leaf axils.	
either broad elliptical & often shiny, or scalelike	Flowers strikingly irregular. 3: The lower petal becomes an enlarged lip or, in *Cypripedium,* a sac. Stamens combined with style and stigma form the "column."	
alternate, with pungent, watery juice, often pinnately lobed or compound	4: Flowers in racemes. Usually 6 stamens, the 2 outer ones short and the 4 inner ones long (or sometimes reduced to 2). Typical of the family is the formation of seedpods while flowering continues. Seedpods contain either one seed or appear pea-podlike with many seeds.	
	5: The exception is one species, *Jussiaea repens,* which has 5 petals and 10 stamens. Color range: light yellow, white, or pink.	
opposite or whorled	All species have very small flowers. Color range: white and pink.	

FAMILY	PETALS OR LOBES	SEPALS	STAMENS	OVARY, PISTIL
REGULAR FLOWERS WITH 5 PETALS OR 5 LOBES				
Malvaceae Mallow Figure 8, p. 111	5 petals	5 united	many (Note 6)	ovary superior pistil compound
Rosaceae Rose Figure 9, p. 111	5 petals usually rounded, standing free	5	many, usually protruding	pistil 1 or more (Note 7)
	These floral parts arranged *around* the ovary (perigynous) instead of above or below. (Note 7)			
Caryophyllaceae Pink Figure 10, p. 111	5 petals frequently notched (Note 8)	5 either separate or united (Note 9)	5–10	ovary superior
Polygonaceae Smartweed Figure 11, p. 112	none	5 petal-like often enlarged into membranes	6–9	ovary superior
Apiaceae (formerly *Umbelliferae*) Parsley Figure 12, p. 112	5 petals	5	5	ovary inferior
Solanaceae Nightshade Figure 13, p. 112	tubular corolla with 5 lobes	5 united	5 inserted in corolla tube	ovary superior
Boraginaceae Borage Figure 14, p. 112	tubular corolla with 5 lobes	5-lobed	5 inserted in tube alternate with lobes	deeply 4-lobed superior ovary; style single

104

LEAVES	OTHER CHARACTERISTICS, REMARKS AND NOTES
usually palmately veined	6: The filaments form a sheath around the style. The many anthers are clustered below the stigma. Flowers often showy. Fruit breaks into pie-shaped sections.
stipules, sometimes winglike, at base of leaf-stems (See picture on page 93, top left)	7: The ovary is surrounded by a cuplike structure, the hypanthium, on which the petals, sepals and stamens appear to be borne. The family is divided into 3 sub-families: 1) Rose-subfamily, mostly herbs; 2) Peach-subfamily, trees and shrubs; and 3) Apple-subfamily, mostly trees.
entire, opposite, narrow, with swollen nodes where stems or leaves emerge	8: All but one genus with general distribution in Missouri have 5 petals, which frequently are notched. One genus, Whitlow Chickweed, Paronychia, has no petals at all. Over half of the Pink family species came from Europe. 9: The sepals of some genera are united and form a long calyx. Color range: white, pink, red.
nodes swollen, covered by a sheath often with a hairy fringe. Sheath completely encircles stem & often is papery.	Flowers in slender spikes, some erect, others nodding. Color range: white, pink, greenish.
generally compound with sheaths at nodes and much divided	The tiny flowers form an umbel, i.e. their stems arise from one point, so that the flowers are arranged in a flat-topped or domed, rounded inflorescence. Eryngium differs both as to inflorescence & leaf shape.
leaves and stems often prickly; leaves mostly alternate	Flowers, pleated (plicate) when in bud, are either star- or bell- or trumpet-shaped tubes of 5 joined petals. In the large genus *Solanum,* the stamens, united around the pistil, protrude beaklike from the corolla.
alternate, usually very hairy or rough (exception: Virginia Bluebells)	Flowers are positioned on a coil which unwinds as blooming progresses.

FAMILY	PETALS OR LOBES	SEPALS	STAMENS	OVARY, PISTIL
REGULAR FLOWERS WITH 5 PETALS OR LOBES (cont'd)				
Ericaceae Heath Figure 17, p. 113	5-lobed corolla (Note 10)	5 united at base	8–10	ovary superior in Rhododendron, inferior in Vaccinium
Convolvulaceae Morning Glory Figure 18, p. 113	5 petals (rarely 4) united into a tube twisted in the bud	5 (rarely 4) united at base	5 inserted deeply in the tube	ovary superior
IRREGULAR FLOWERS WITH 5 PETALS OR LOBES				
Scrophulariaceae Figwort Figure 15, p. 112	5 lobes (Notes 11, 12)	5 lobed	usually 4 with a sterile upper 5th (Note 13)	ovary superior
Lamiaceae (formerly *Labiatae*) Mint Figure 16, p. 112	corolla with 2 lips (Note 14)	5 fused	4 (Note 15)	ovary superior
	* Square-stemmed plants are NOT necessarily members of this family.			
Fabaceae (formerly *Leguminosae*) Pea Figure 19, p. 113 (Note 16)	5 lowest 2 often joined	5 united at base	many, often fused in groups	fruit a "legume," i.e. a pod, containing many seeds in a bean or peapod; fruit splits into 2 sections, seed attached to one edge

LEAVES	OTHER CHARACTERISTICS, REMARKS AND NOTES
alternate	10: The two Missouri genera, *Rhododendron* (Azalea) and *Vaccinium* (Blueberry), have very different floral arrearance. *Ericaceae* are indicators of acid soils. Color range: white, pink, greenish.
alternate	Trailing and twining vines. The flowers are only lightly lobed. Color range: white, pink, blue, sometimes with red throat. Fruit consists of 3 or 4 large seeds.
alternate or opposite or whorled	11: Most species have 5 lobes of the corolla, but the genus *Scrophularia* has only 3. 12: Flowers of most species have long, swollen, tubular corollas and are irregular, but others (e.g. *Verbascum*) have nearly regular flowers and the tube is very short. 13: As in the Mint Family, 2 stamens are often longer than the other 2. — In the genus *Penstemon,* a 5th stamen is converted into a hairy stem without pollen-bearing organ (anther), apparently to attract insects.
most have square stems* & aromatic green parts, opposite leaves	14: Flowers, either in spikes or clustered ball-like in leaf axils, are 2-lipped. The upper lip with 2 lobes, the lower lip 3-lobed or divided. 15: The tube usually holds 4 stamens of which 2 are on long filaments and fertile, while the other 2 are on shorter filaments and either fertile or sterile or missing in several species. Color range: pink, white, magenta
generally compound with either many leaflets or with 3 leaflets (trifoliate) as in clover, alternate (but leaflets may be opposite) with stipules (see picture on page 93, top left)	16: The family is divided into 3 sub-families: *Papilionoideae.* By far the most important sub-family, comprising most genera and species. Of the 5 petals, the lower 2 form the "keel," the 2 lateral ones are the "wings," and the large upper one is the "banner" or "standard" or "sail." *Mimosoideae.* Mimosalike tufts or balls of tiny, regular flowers. Two genera are widespread in Missouri: *Schrankia* and *Desmanthus.* *Caesalpinioideae.* Flowers in this small sub-family are nearly regular as in the genus *Cassia* (senna).

FAMILY	PETALS OR LOBES	SEPALS	STAMENS	OVARY, PISTIL
Violaceae Violet Figure 20, p. 113	5 petals, the lowest forms a spur (Note 17)	5	5 anthers form a cone-shaped cluster about the base of the pistil	floral parts attached around the ovary (perigynous)
SPECIAL FLORAL ARRANGEMENTS				
Asclepiadaceae Milkweed Figure 21, p. 113	5 petals turned down- ward (Note 18)	5 small, also turned downward	5 united with a central stigma	
Asteraceae (formerly *Compositae)* Daisy Figure 22, p. 114	By far the largest family in North America and Missouri. Many small flowers (also called florets) are inserted in the expanded end of the flower-stalk, which is known as the receptacle. The receptacle is enclosed and supported by from one to many rows of small, leaflike bracts, which, collectively, form the involucre. The florets of one receptacle are referred to as the "flowerhead," of which there are three types: Note 19.			
Euphorbiaceae Spurge Figure 23, p. 114	Floral appearance often insignificant. The genus *Euphorbia* produces a floral cup, known as the cyathium. Inserted in this cup are male flowers and one female flower on the top of a stalk (gynophore). After fertilization, the swollen ovary protrudes from the cyathium.			
Ranunculaceae Buttercup Figure 24, p. 114 (Note 20)	none to indefinite	5 or more, often replace petals	many, arranged spirally	pistils and ovaries numerous, superior

108

LEAVES	OTHER CHARACTERISTICS, REMARKS AND NOTES	
shapes very variable	17: Flowers of the genus *Viola* can be white, yellow, blue, purple, violet or mixtures of these colors. The genus *Hybanthus,* the Green Violet, has only one species in the U.S.A. See pp. 52, 179.	
leaves opposite or whorled, entire	18: A most unusual flower structure: the 5 petals and 5 sepals are bent downward, forming the base for a cup called the "corona." consisting of the "hood" and 5 "horns," which bend inward toward 5 united stamens and a central stigma. The pollen is united into a pollen-mass, the "pollinia." Plants contain a milky, poisonous juice.	**109**

19: 1) Straplike ray flowers ONLY. This group is called the *Ligulaceae* (from *ligulum,* Latin, "strap"). Examples: Dandelion and Chickory. Members of this group contain a milky juice.

2) Disk flowers ONLY (NO ray flowers). Individual flowers are tubular with a 5-pointed rim. The 5 stamens are attached to the stigma by their anthers. The stigma is usually 2-lobed. Examples: Thistle, Ironweed, Kansas Gay-feather.

3) BOTH disk AND ray flowers. The ray flowers may be pointed, rounded or square, with or without (normally) 5 teeth. The ray flowers are often sterile. Example: Daisy, Sunflower.

The green parts of plants belonging to the genus *Euphorbia* contain a milky juice, which is also present in many species of other genera in the family. Juice is poisonous and may cause a rash. White, small petal-like appendages (usually 5) are common in the family. Only one native species of the genus *Euphorbia* has showy, white appendages of the floral cup, which simulate petals — *Euphorbia corollata.*

variable, often palmate, deeply dissected; basal leaves often differ from stem leaves	20: Flower shapes in this family vary greatly: 1) Flowers irregular, with spurs or claws (*Delphinium, Aquilegia*). 2) Flowers without petals, the sepals substituting for them (*Hepatica, Anemonella, Anemone*). Flowers generally irregular due to variable number of sepals. 3) Flowers WITH petals and sepals, normally 5 of each, but frequently more (*Ranunculus*). 4) Flowers with petals and sepals, but the sepals drop when the blossoms open *(Actaea).* 5) Flowers without petals whose sepals drop on opening (*Hydrastis, Cimicifuga, Thalictrum*). 6) Flowers which are either male or female *(Thalictrum).*

110

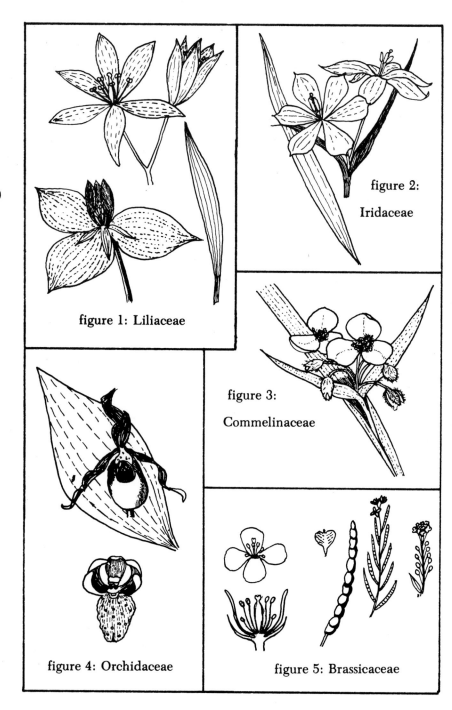

figure 1: Liliaceae

figure 2:
Iridaceae

figure 3:
Commelinaceae

figure 4: Orchidaceae

figure 5: Brassicaceae

figure 6: Onagraceae

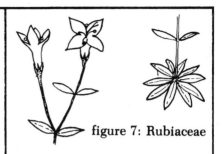

figure 7: Rubiaceae

111

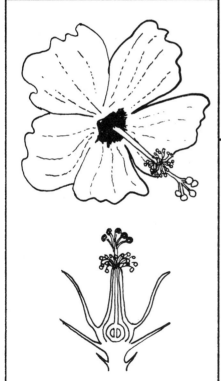

figure 9: Rosaceae

figure 8: Malvaceae

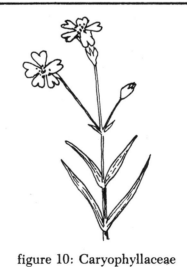

figure 10: Caryophyllaceae

112

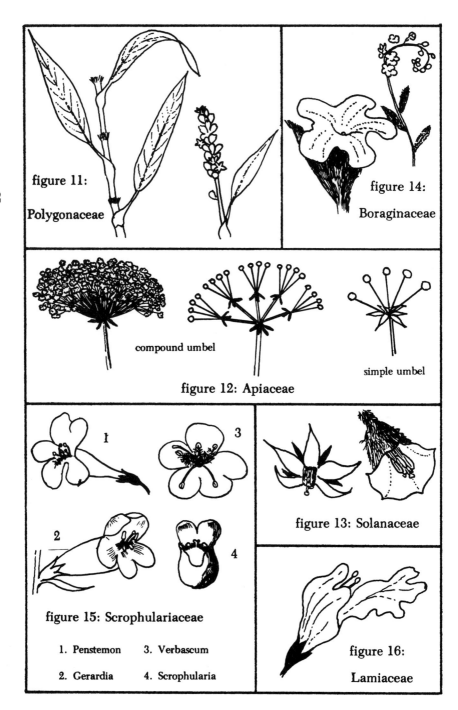

figure 11:

Polygonaceae

figure 14:

Boraginaceae

compound umbel

simple umbel

figure 12: Apiaceae

1

3

2

4

figure 13: Solanaceae

figure 15: Scrophulariaceae

1. Penstemon   3. Verbascum

2. Gerardia   4. Scrophularia

figure 16:

Lamiaceae

figure 17: Ericaceae

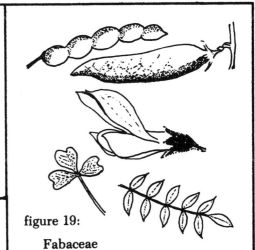

figure 19:
Fabaceae

113

figure 18: Convolvulaceae

figure 21: Asclepiadaceae

Viola

Hybanthus

figure 20: Violaceae

114

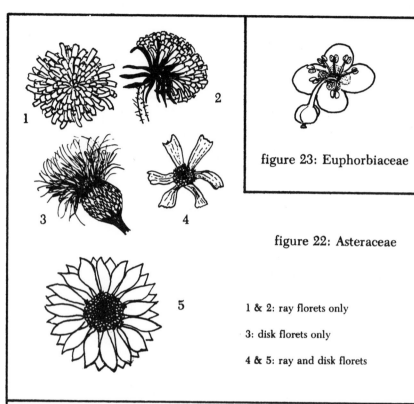

figure 23: Euphorbiaceae

figure 22: Asteraceae

1 & 2: ray florets only

3: disk florets only

4 & 5: ray and disk florets

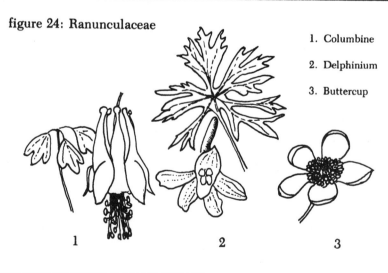

figure 24: Ranunculaceae

1. Columbine

2. Delphinium

3. Buttercup

Class: MONOCOTYLEDONS

Monocots are plants whose embryo has only one seed-leaf or cotyledon. Flower parts in threes or multiples of three. Leaves with unbranched, parallel veins from base to tip of leaf (except *Trillium* and *Arum* genera).

ARUM FAMILY *Araceae*

115

Arisaema atrorubens [57]   Jack-in-the-Pulpit, Indian Turnip

In rich woods, statewide. Blooms from April to June.

Plant averages 18″ (45 cm) high, but specimens to 2½ feet (76 cm) can be found.

Preacher Jack, the club-like spadix to which the tiny flowers are attached, stands in the pulpit with an overhanging canopy. The hood may be purplish-brown, purple-bronze with pale green stripes, or entirely pale green.

Leaves are on long stems, mostly 2 or 3-divided, dull green.

The fruit consists of clustered berries which turn from a shiny green to brilliant scarlet.

Indians ate the starchy root which is poisonous unless thoroughly dried.

Arisaema, Greek, from *aris* and *haema* or "Aris-blood;" *atrorubens*, Latin, "deep red" from the color of the hood.

Arisaema dracontium [53]   Green Dragon

On rich, moist, usually level ground in woods, statewide. Blooms from April to June.

A tall plant, occasionally to 3 feet (90 cm).

The lower part of the flower is wrapped tightly by a green sheet from which the long, tail-like spadix—the dragon—arises.

The leaves are divided into 5 to 15 large, lance-shaped leaflets (compared to 3 segments for the Jack-in-the-Pulpit).

The fruits, clustered around the spadix, turn from green to shiny, scarlet berries.

The root is a rounded corm, flattened at top and bottom, often quite large. Indians dried these corms and used them for food.

Arisaema, Greek, from *aris* and *haema* or "Aris-blood;" *dracontium*, Latin, "of the dragons," as the deeply divided leaves are reminiscent of dragon's claws.

SPIDERWORT FAMILY *Commelinaceae*

Commelina communis [88]   Day-flower

In low woods, waste ground, bottomlands, often around dwellings, statewide. Blooms from May to October. Native of Asia.

Plants 12″ to 2 feet (30 to 60 cm).

The flowers emerge, one at a time, from a large, folded, keel-like sheath. There are two large blue petals, like flags, above and a third, much smaller and green or green-white, nearly hidden below the reproductive parts of the flower. The male parts, anthers, are in two entirely different shapes—3 on short stems with lobed appendages and 3 on longer stems with claw-shaped pollen parts. The 3 on short stems are sterile.

Leaves clasp the stem, are narrow, lance-shaped, pointed, and parallel veined.

Commelina, for Commelin, an early Dutch botanist; *communis,* Latin for "common."

There are several other species of Commelina in Missouri, all with similar characteristics.

116

Tradescantia ohiensis [86]   Spiderwort, Reflexed Spiderwort

On prairies, waste places, along roads and railroads statewide, except extreme northwest and southeast. Blooms from May to July.

A common roadside plant to 3 feet (90 cm) tall.

Flowers in clusters but only one or two open at one time. Size of 3 petals varies and flower may be from ¾″ to 1½″ (2 to 4 cm) across. The 3 pointed petals give the flower a triangular shape. The stamens are bearded and fluffy. Color is clear blue or rose or purplish-lavender. White flowers have been reported but are very rare.

Leaves 12″ (30 cm) long, narrow and folded lengthwise. They are distinctly blue-green and clasp the stem in a thick node.

Tradescantia, for John Tradescant, gardener to Charles I of England in the early 17th century.

There are seven other species of *Tradescantia* in Missouri, all similar to T. ohiensis. T. species do cross and produce hybrids, sometimes making proper identification difficult.

Tradescantia virginiana   Early Spiderwort

In dry, open woods, on slopes or in valleys, generally on acid soil, in eastern Missouri. Blooms late April to June.

Many 3-petalled flowers clustered in a showy display. Each flower lasts only one day. Individual flowers to 1½" (4 cm) across. Flower stalks (peduncles) and bracts are hairy with gland-tipped hair (smooth in *T. ohiensis*). On sunny days the flowers close by noon.

Leaves, reminiscent of Iris, to ¾" (2 cm) wide.

Tradescantia subaspera   Zigzag Spiderwort

In rich woods, bottomland, near streams, generally on lime soil, in central and east-central Missouri. Blooms June to September.

This late-blooming *Tradescantia* grows to 2½ feet (76 cm) tall. It has fairly small flowers atop many-leaved stems which change direction, or "zig-zag," between leaf-nodes.

117

Tradescantia longipes [83]   Spiderwort, Wild Crocus

On wooded slopes and valleys with acid soils in the Ozark region. Blooms in April and May.

A low plant, 6" to 8" (15 to 20 cm) tall.

Flowers triangular with 3 pointed petals. The stamens have a fuzzy, hairy fringe which gives the flower an attractive center. Color is magenta or purple to purplish-blue, but always very bright.

Leaves are basal and grass-like, about 7" (18 cm) long and ½" (12 mm) wide, "creased" along the center vein.

This flower is not found outside Missouri.

Tradescantia, for John Tradescant, gardener to Charles I of England in the early 17th century; *longipes*, Latin, *longus* for "long" and *pes* for "foot or stalk." The reason for the species name is uncertain.

LILY FAMILY *Liliacae*

Allium stellatum [75]   Wild Onion

On limestone glades and ledges of southern Missouri, except southeast and western counties. Blooms from July to November.

One of the two fall-blooming Wild Onions with showy, pink, sometimes white, flowers on stalks up to 12" (30 cm) high. Flowers are produced in umbels.

Narrow leaves grow from the base of the plant.

Wild Onions and Garlics grow from bulbs.

The strong onion smell from any crushed part of the plant is unmistakable.

Allium, the classical Latin name for Garlic; *stellatum*, Latin for "star-shaped," referring to the flowers.

Allium canadense Wild Garlic

In moist places, statewide. Blooms from May to July.

Plants 8″ to 24″ (20 to 60 cm) tall.

Flowers white, or, instead of flowers, it produces clusters of bulblets (little bulbs) which drop to the ground and root.

Leaves on lower ⅓ of stalk narrow.

Allium mutabile Wild Onion

On prairies, glades, limestone exposures, absent from north and southeast Missouri. Blooms from late April to June.

118 Flower colors variable, from rose, pink, or lilac, to nearly white. Similar to A. *canadense* but with flowers only, no bulblets.

Camassia scilloides [10] Wild Hyacinth

On prairies, rocky slopes, ledges, low rich woods, absent from northeast and southeast lowlands. Blooms from early April to mid-May.

Fragrant, bluish-white flowers—as many as 20—grow on a long flower stalk to 2 feet (60 cm) high.

Basal leaves are narrow, less than ½″ (12 mm) wide, and taper to a point.

The bulb is edible and was gathered by the Indians.

The botanical name *Camassia* and the English "Camas" are derived from the Indian word *Quamash; scilloides* indicates that *Cammasia* looks like a *Scilla*, one of our early blooming garden flowers.

Erythronium albidum [3] Dog-tooth Violet, Trout Lily

In low, rich woods along streams, statewide. Blooms from March to May.

The white to bluish-white flowers on stems about 7″ (18 cm) tall have 3 petals and 3 sepals which look nearly alike. When the flower is closed the parts are straight, but as they open they recurve.

Leaves are to 6″ (15 cm) long, elliptical, and cover extensive areas in early spring. Most of the leaves, which are strongly mottled with brown and have a silvery covering on the under surface, are single and no flowers appear with them. The flowers arise only from 2-leaved plants. It is not known whether the single-leaf plants are immature or sterile. In the East the plant is called "Thousandleaf" because there are so many leaves and so few flowers.

The plant is a true Lily, arising from a bulb. It takes four years for flowers to develop from seed.

Erythronium, Greek for "red," since a red European species gave the genus its name; *albidum*, Latin for "white."

Erythronium americanum   Yellow Dog-tooth Violet

In rich woods and wooded bottomlands, scattered south of the Missouri River. Blooms March to May.

The yellow flowers are somewhat larger than those of *E. albidum,* as are the blotched leaves.

Hemerocallis fulva [39]   Day Lily

Along roads and railroads, abandoned homes, waste areas, scattered statewide. Blooms from May to August. Native of Eurasia.

The large, orange, lily-like flowers have 3 petals and 3 sepals which look much alike. The open flowers spread to about 3″ (8 cm) and are **119** carried on long, slender, round stalks without leaves to about 3 feet (90 cm) high.

Leaves are basal, narrow and strap-like, to about 2 feet (60 cm) long.

The Day Lily is said to have been brought here by the clipper ships, though it may have been introduced from Europe, and was planted extensively all over the country. This immigrant is sterile and all the millions of plants from coast to coast came from root divisions. With thousands of fertile hybrids available, it is amazing that none of them have escaped into the wild from cultivation.

The flowers are rich in protein and are eaten in China. The roots are said to taste like Salsify.

Neither insects nor diseases plague the plant.

Hemerocallis, Greek for "beauty for one evening," since each flower lasts only one day; *fulva,* Latin for "yellow." The original Day Lily opens in the afternoon and closes the next morning.

Lilium michiganense [44]   Turk's Cap Lily, Michigan Lily

In low woods, prairie swales, swampy meadows statewide except southeast lowlands. Blooms mid-June to mid-July.

Plants to 3 feet (90 cm) tall.

Flower stalks arise from a common leaf axil on plant stalk. The orange flowers with many purple-brown dots first spread open and later recurve. Petals and sepals, 3 of each, look alike. The long-stemmed stamens and the style protrude from the perianth. Flowers point downward.

Lance-shaped leaves, parallel veined and to 1″ (25 mm) wide, are arranged in whorls around the plant stem with from 4 to 10 leaves in one circle.

This is the only Lily native to Missouri.

Lilium, Latin, the classical name for Lilies.

Nothoscordum bivalve [4]   False Garlic

On glades, ledges, upland wooded areas, along streams in south and central Missouri. Blooms from March to May, sometimes again in the fall.
Flower stalks without leaves to 10″ (25 cm) high with an umbel of white or yellowish-white flowers, each with 3 petals and 3 sepals which look alike.
Leaves string-like and lower than the flower cluster.
The plant has the bulb root common to the Lily Family. Though it looks like an Onion or Garlic it does not have the characteristic odor.
Nothoscordum, Greek for "false garlic;" *bivalve*, Latin for "two-valved," referring to the subtended umbel.

Ornithogalum umbellatum [12]   Star of Bethlehem

In fields, along roads, varied, in southwest, central, and northeast Missouri.
Ornithogolum is an aggressive colonizer and can be expected to have spread into many new localities and counties. Blooms from April to June. Native of Europe.
Forms dense clumps with many leaves and flower stalks. Flowers are clustered in umbels—therefore *umbellatum*—on stems to 12″ (30 cm) high. The 3 petals and 3 sepals which form the "star" are silvery white above, white with green lines below.
The leaves are grass-like, rolled inward, very dark green. The central vein is white.
A bulbous plant, it produces bulbs at an incredible rate. Often seen in gardens. **The plant is poisonous.**
Ornithogalum, Greek for "bird's milk," but the connection isn't known.

Polygonatum commutatum [15]   Solomon's Seal

In rich or rocky woods, stream banks, along roads and railroads statewide. Blooms May to June.
Usually about 3 feet (90 cm) tall, but stem can be up to 6 feet (1.8 m).
Short stems with a cluster of 2 to 10 flowers arise from leaf axils. Flowers are slender, cylindrical, about 1″ (2.5 cm) long, which hang bell-like.
Along the upper portion of the curving stem are alternate, ovate leaves, parallel veined, each clasping the plant stem. Leaves are about 2″ (5 cm) wide and to 5″ (13 cm) long.
Fruit is a blue berry.
Solomon's Seal refers to the wound "sealing" properties of the plant, according to Dioscorides, a 1st century writer.
Polygonatum, Greek for "with many knees," referring to the thick, hori-

zontal rootstock which has circular scars, the scars of former stalks; *commutatum*, Latin for "changing."

Smilacina racemosa [14]   False Solomon's Seal, False Spikenard

In rich woods statewide. Blooms May to June.

Normally unbranched, arching stalk with a slight zig-zag effect, 2 to 3 feet (60 to 90 cm) tall.

The tiny, creamy-white flowers grow in a plume-like cluster at the top of the stalk.

Leaves, almost without stems, are alternate along the stalk, lance-shaped, conspicuously parallel veined. The leaves of False Solomon's Seal resemble Solomon's Seal, but the flower arrangement of the two plants is totally different.

Smilacina, Greek, "resembling Smilax," a large group in the Lily Family; *racemosa*, Latin for "flowering in a raceme" or cluster.

121

Trillium sessile [58]   Wake Robin, Trillium

On wooded slopes and bottomlands in rich soil; common south and scattered north of the Missouri River. Blooms April to early June.

On a simple, bare stalk is a whorl of evenly spaced leaves forming a 3-pointed star from 8″ to 12″ (20 to 30 cm) above the ground.

The flower's 3 petals stand upright to 2″ (5 cm) high. Their coloring is variable—brown-purple, maroon, brick red, or mixed with dull green. They may also be greenish-yellow, brownish-yellow, or greenish.

The leaves are ovate, pointed, without stems (sessile), dark green, and may or may not be mottled.

Trillium, Latin from *tri* and *lilium* for "three" and "lily," because leaves and flower parts are in threes; *sessile*, Latin, "without leaf stalks."

Trillium recurvatum   Purple Trillium

In rich woods, rarely in open grassy areas, of east and south Missouri. Blooms in April and May.

Very similar to *T. sessile*, but the sepals curve downward on mature flowers. It is the commonest Trillium in the east-central part of the state.

Trillium flexipes [7] *(gleasoni)*   White Wake Robin, White Trillium

On rich wooded slopes and bottomlands, ravines, in east and east-central Missouri. Blooms in April and May.

A large, white Trillium standing to 2 feet (60 cm) tall.

The flower, to 2½″ (6.5 cm) across, appears on a long extension of the plant stem, either in horizontal or drooping position when in full bloom. The 3 large petals are white while the 3 narrow sepals are green.

The 3 whorled leaves are heart-shaped, pointed, usually as broad as long, to 9″ (23 cm). They are not mottled.

Trillium, Latin from *tri* and *lilium* for "three" and "lily," because leaves and flower parts are in threes; *flexipes*, Latin, "flexible foot," probably referring to the nodding flower.

122 *Trillium viride*   Green Trillium

On wooded slopes or in full sun in valleys of southwest and east-central Missouri. Blooms in April and May.

The green petals are longer than those of *T. sessile*. The color ranges from light green to yellow.

Leaves are broadly heart-shaped.

Uvularia grandiflora [32]   Bellwort

On rich wooded slopes or valleys statewide, except some southwest counties. Blooms in April and May.

The smooth stem, to 2 feet (60 cm) tall, is usually forked. After flowering the plant stem elongates, producing a zig-zag pattern between the leaf nodes.

The nodding, yellow flowers are about 2″ (5 cm) long with 3 petals and 3 sepals which look alike.

Bright green leaves, downy underneath, completely enfold the stem at their base.

Uvularia, from Latin *uvula*, a small, conical body in the center of the human palate which the flower resembles; *grandiflora*, Latin for "large-flowered."

Yucca smalliana [23]   Spanish Bayonet, Adam's Needle

Along roads, railroads, and embankments, scattered statewide. Blooms from May to August. Native of southern United States, introduced into Missouri.

The sinous flower stalks grows up to 7 feet (2.1 m) tall and is loaded with creamy-white flowers on numerous branches off the main stalk. The flowers are about 2″ (5 cm) across with 3 petals and 3 sepals which look identical. They form a cup.

The leaves are the "Spanish bayonets"—narrow, hard, sharply spiked, to 2 feet (60 cm) long. They grow in great quantities in a basal rosette. The fruit is a large, papery capsule, about 3″ (8 cm) long, which contains hundreds of flat, black seeds in compartments.

Only one insect is capable of fertilizing the *Yucca*—the Pronuba moth. It lays its eggs in the ovary and the emerging larvae consume some, but not all, of the developing seeds. A Missouri entomologist, Charles V. Riley, discovered this unique interrelation between plant and insect.

Yucca, an Indian name erroneously applied to this plant; *smalliana*, for John Kunkel Small, 1869-1938.

AMARYLLIS FAMILY *Amaryllidaceae* 123

Agave virginica [55] American Aloe, False Aloe, Rattlesnake Master

On rocky glades, dry uplands, occasionally along streams, in either lime or acid soils; in the Ozark region north to St. Louis County. Blooms from June to August.

A strange looking plant of usually dry situations. A straight, slender stem arises to about 6 feet (1.8), rarely higher, from a rosette of basal leaves.

On the top area of the stem emerge small, green and brown, tube-shaped flowers from which protrude the pollen-bearing anthers. The flowers are fragrant with a scent reminiscent of Easter Lilies.

The leaves of the basal rosette are thick, dark green, lance-shaped and pointed, with minute teeth along the edges.

This is Missouri's lone representative of a desert-dwelling clan.

Agave is Greek for "admirable."

Hypoxis hirsuta [31] Yellow Star Grass

On prairies, meadows, glades, open woods in acid soils statewide except southeast lowlands. Flowers in April and May, sometimes in fall.

The flowers may open when the stem is only 2″ (5 cm) above the ground, but in later spring the flowers are carried on thread-like, very hairy stems to 6″ (15 cm) tall.

Flowers have 3 petals and 3 sepals which look alike, bright yellow above, greenish and very hairy below, with 1 to 3 flowers on a stem.

Grass-like leaves and the yellow flowers explain the common name, Yellow Star Grass.

The root is a corm.

Hypoxis, Greek from *hypo* and *oxys* for "below" and "sharp," because the seed pod tapers toward its base; *hirsuta*, Latin, "hairy."

IRIS FAMILY *Iridaceae*

Belamcanda chinensis [50]   Blackberry Lily

In rocky open woods and glades, scattered statewide. Blooms in July and August.

Flowers have 3 petals and 3 petal-like sepals of light orange color, spotted with crimson, on very tall stalks, sometimes over 3 feet tall (1 m).

The leaves can hardly be distinguished from those of the German Iris, or common garden Iris.

Blackberry Lily gets its name from the shiny, black seeds which look surprisingly like blackberries and remain on the stalks for many weeks.

124   This strange plant was brought to this country by clipper ships, probably from China. It cannot stand competition from other plants and finds refuge on barren, rocky slopes of open woods and glades. It is a favorite in the yards of Ozarkians.

Belamcanda is believed to be an East Indian name.

Iris virginica [85]   Southern Blue Flag

In wet meadows, swamps, river bottoms, ditches of northern and central Missouri, scattered elsewhere. Blooms from May to early July.

The Iris is one of the most beautiful wildflowers of Missouri. The flowers are carried on stems to 3 feet (90 cm) tall which rise above the many leaves. The "falls," as the 3 wide sepals are descriptively called, as well as the 3 petals or "standards," are violet over a white base. Many variations in coloring appear, from a bluish-white to deep violet. The falls are veined in deeper tones.

Leaves are strap-like, narrow and over 2 feet (60 cm) long.

Of the four native Iris, this has the widest distribution. "Drainage improvements" and land developments are eliminating its habitat.

Iris, Greek for "rainbow" because the genus includes species in many colors.

Nemastylis geminiflora [84]   Nemastylis, Celestial Lily

On limestone glades and rocky slopes of eastern Missouri. Blooms from late April to mid-May.

Plants to about 12″ (30 cm) high.

Flowers up to 2½″ (6.5 cm) across, each a six-pointed star in a delicate blue-violet color.

Leaves, 3 or 4, long and folded, very narrow and clasping the stem.

The root is a bulb—often found deep below the surface in sticky clay.

Though not common, it is sometimes found in large colonies on glades shaded by junipers.

Nemastylis, Greek for "thread-like styles;" *geminiflora,* Latin, means "twin-flowered" because two flowers emerge from each spathe, a leaf-like bract which surrounds the inflorescence.

Sisyrinchium campestre [81]   Prairie Blue-eyed Grass

In rocky, open woods and glades, in grassy places, statewide. Blooms from April to June.

To 2 feet (60 cm) tall, but usually much lower.

Flowers are small, blue, six-pointed stars on flat, two-sided stems. A white flowering form grows in southwestern counties, and a rare yellow form also exists.

Below each flower cluster are two grass-like bracts. The basal leaves are also grasslike and stand stiff and upright.

Sisyrinchium is an old Greek name; *campestre,* Latin for "of the field."

125

Sisyrinchium bermudiana   Pointed Blue-eyed Grass

In moist soils of woodlands and valleys, scattered statewide. Blooms from May to July.

Branched, with wider leaves than *S. campestre.* Stems conspicuously winged.

ORCHID FAMILY *Orchidaceae*

Cypripedium calceolus [34]   Yellow Lady-slipper

In acid soils on upper parts of wooded slopes facing north or east, statewide. Blooms from late April to early June.

Two varieties of this Lady-slipper are found in Missouri. Variety *parviflorum* (small-flowered) grows in western and southern counties while the larger variety, *pubescens* (hairy), to 2 feet (60 cm) tall, adorns eastern counties.

Cypripedium blossoms are unique with their bright yellow sac-like "slipper," actually a specialized petal. The long, brown, twisted "flags," one upright and one to either side of the "slipper," are sepals. Fertilization, mostly by bees, demands that the insect follow a labyrinthine obstacle course.

The broad leaves, parallel veined, clasp the stem. They are 6″ (15 cm) long, pointed and hairy.

Cypripedium, from Greek Kypris, the counterpart of Venus, and *pedium,* "shoe"—thus Venus' slipper; *calceolus,* Latin for "with a spur."

Spiranthes cernua [28]   Ladies' Tresses

On limestone glades, upland dry prairies, wet meadows south of the Missouri River, scattered north. Blooms from August to November.

This is one Orchid in Missouri which can be found in stands of hundreds. Small, white flowers, about ⅛" (8 mm) long, are arranged in a spiral around the stem which grows to 18" (45 cm) tall. The flowers are commonly strongly fragrant, but not always. The perfume is that of Lily of the Valley or of vanilla extract.

There are a few narrow, alternate leaves clasping the flower stem. The grass-like basal leaves have disappeared by flowering time.

Spiranthes, Greek, referring to the twisted spikes; *cernua,* Latin, "drooping" or "nodding."

126

Class: DICOTYLEDONS

Dicots are plants whose embryo has two seed-leaves—cotyledons. Flower parts are usually in fours or fives or multiples thereof. Leaves have a network of branching veins.

BIRTHWORT FAMILY *Aristolochiaceae*

Asarum canadense [57]   Wild Ginger

On rich, wooded slopes, moist valleys, bottom of ravines statewide except southeast lowlands and a few extreme western counties. Blooms in April and May.

A low-growing, hairy plant, about 6" (15 cm) high, spreading from creeping underground stems.

The flowers are hidden by the leaves and arise from the axils of the leaf stalks. They are three-parted, a rich red-brown with delicate designs and stiff, white hair. Apparently the flowers attract carrion-eating insects, thus the color and design.

Leaves are large, heart-shaped, strongly veined, leathery, with a shiny surface.

The fleshy roots are dense and intertwined and have a distinct aroma of ginger. They have been used as a ginger substitute.

Asarum, Greek, the ancient name of the European species.

BUCKWHEAT FAMILY *Polygonaceae*

Polygonum coccineum [74]   Water Smartweed, Shoestring Smartweed

On margins of lakes, swamps, sloughs, streams, in ditches, statewide except some Ozark counties. Blooms from June to October.

Rank plants to 4 feet (1.2 m) tall with rose to rose-red flowers in tight cylindrical spikes.

Leaves on short stems, elliptical, to 6″ (15 cm) long.

The seeds are a very important food for ducks.

Smartweed gets its name from the peppery taste of the leaves.

Polygonum, Greek, "many knees," from the knob-like swelling where leaves or branches emerge from main stems; *coccineum,* Latin, "red" or "pink."

127

Polygonum persicaria   Lady's Thumb

In moist or wet habitats, widely distributed. Blooms from May to October.

Smooth, not hairy. Stems reddish.

Tight, spike-like flower clusters, held upright, are pink, dull rose-purplish, or white.

Leaves often with purplish, brownish, or dark green splotches.

Look for a papery sheath, which is fringed, at each joint.

Polygonum sagittatum   Arrow-leaved Tear-thumb

In moist or wet habitats, widely distributed. Blooms from June to October.

Small, dense flower clusters, pink or white.

Leaves narrow, arrow-shaped, with weak prickles on lower midrib. Leaves far apart, sometimes blunt-pointed.

Called Tear-thumb because of the hooked prickles that line the four angles of the stems.

Polygonum pensylvanicum   Pinkweed

In moist or wet habitats, widely distributed. Blooms from May to October.

Branching and sprawling.

Flowers in long clusters, pink, sometimes white.

Lance-shaped shiny leaves.

Without prickles, joints sometimes red. Look for gland-tipped hairs on upper branches and stems.

Polygonum lapathifolium   Pale Smartweed

In moist or wet habitats, widely distributed. Blooms from June to November.

Flower clusters arching or drooping. Flowers greenish-white or pink. Sheaths at joints not hairy.

Polygonum punctatum   Water Smartweed

In moist or wet habitats, usually standing in water, widely distributed. Blooms from July to November.
Flower clusters erect or slightly drooping, greenish-white.
Floral envelope (calyx) and leaves conspicuously dotted.

Polygonum hydropiperoides   Wild Water Pepper

128   In moist or wet habitats, widely distributed. Blooms from June to November.
Slender, sparse flower spikes, more or less interrupted. Color off-white or pink.
Sheaths at joints have fringe of slender bristles.

Polygonum virginianum   Virginia Knotweed

In rich woodlands statewide. Blooms from July to October.
Grows to 4 feet (1.5 m) tall.
Flowers tiny, greenish or pink, spaced far apart on slender spikes, often 10″ (25 cm) long.
Leaves large, ovate.
Fringed sheaths at joints.

Polygonum tenue   Slender Knotweed

On dry, acid soils of the Ozarks. Blooms from June to October.
An annual with four-angled, slender stems, much branched, to 12″ (30 cm) long.
Flowers insignificant in the leaf axils.
Leaves linear and erect, to only 1″ (2 cm) long.

Polygonum scandens [26]   Climbing False Buckwheat

On moist, low ground, alluvial valleys, floodplains, statewide. Flowers from July to November.
A rampant climber often forming curtain-like masses of twining growth with distinctly red stems.
Flowers minute, but produced in such quantities on leafy flower spikes that the effect is showy. Flowers are green-white, sometimes pink. The flower envelope (calyx) is five-parted. The outer three segments are strongly winged, contributing much to the overall flower cluster.
Leaves to 6″ (15 cm) long, are either heart- or arrow-shaped.

Fruit winged, with jet black, shiny seeds which look and taste similar to Buckwheat.

Polygonum, Greek, "many knees," from the knob-like swelling where leaves or branches emerge from main stems; *scandens,* Latin, "climbing."

Rumex altissimus [52]   Tall, False, or Peach-leaved Dock

In fields, waste places, alluvial ground along streams, mostly north of the Missouri River but scattered elsewhere. Blooms in April and May.

A stoutly stemmed, erect, perennial plant, from 2 to 4 feet (.6 to 1.2 m) tall, either unbranched or with few branches.

Flowers are very numerous, minute, in densely spaced whorls, carried in a loose, irregular inflorescence called a panicled raceme.

129

Leaves alternate on stems, pointed at both ends, are to 10″ (25 cm) long near base and are flat and smooth-edged, without the wrinkles and wavy margins of other Docks.

Fruit is a winged seed with heart-shaped wings. Seeds of Docks were used by Indians to make a meal for bread.

The plants and fruit turn a rich red-brown after flowering and become a conspicuous sight in the landscape. The pollen is carried by wind and contributes to the discomfort of hay fever sufferers.

Rumex is the Roman name for Dock; *altissimus,* Latin, "highest" or "very high."

There are 13 species of Rumex found in Missouri, but only three have wide distribution. Differences in the flowers are indistinguishable.

Rumex acetosella   Sheep Sorrel

In waste places statewide. Blooms from May to September. Native of Europe.

Similar to *R. altissimus,* but leaves are arrow-shaped.

Rumex crispus.   Sour Dock

In waste places statewide. Blooms in April and May. Native of Europe.
Leaves are long, conspicuously wavy and wrinkled.

FOUR-O'CLOCK FAMILY *Nyctaginaceae*

Mirabilis nyctaginea [66]   Wild Four-o'clock

On prairies, waste places, along roads and railroads statewide. Blooms from May to October.

The branched plants with reddish colored stems grow to 2 feet (60 cm) tall.

The pink to light purple flowers are bell-shaped and face upward in terminal clusters which arise out of a green, five-lobed involucre.

Leaves are heart-shaped or triangular to oval, to about 3½" (9 cm) long, opposite, on stems.

Four-o'clock refers to the flower's characteristic of opening in the afternoon.

Mirabilis, Latin for "strange" or "wonderful;" *nyctaginea,* Greek for "resembling Nyctago," a member of the same Family.

Mirabilis albida   Pale Umbrella Wort

130 On bluffs, glades, prairies, open places, statewide except northeast counties. Blooms from May to October.

Flowers pinkish to white-lilac.

Leaves narrow, lanceolate, opposite.

POKEWEED FAMILY *Phytolaccaceae*

Phytolacca americana [53]   Pokeweed

On waste ground, farm lots, fields, along roads and railroads statewide. Blooms from May to October.

Purplish, thick, much branched stems to 10 feet (3 m) tall.

Small, greenish-white flowers in racemes on white stalks. Each flower ¼" (5 mm) across with 5 white sepals and a rounded ovary.

Leaves are oblong, smooth, pointed at both ends, on short stems.

Fruits are dark purple berries eaten by birds and wildfowl. The juice of the berries is used as food coloring and as ink.

The root has medicinal qualities and some people eat young shoots of the plant.

Phytolacca is from the Greek *phyto* meaning "plant" and *lacca,* a reference to the red juice of the berries which resembles the red juice obtained from an insect *(Tachardia lacca)* used for dye.

PURSLANE FAMILY *Portulacaceae*

Claytonia virginica [1]   Spring Beauty

In open woods, prairies, meadows statewide. Blooms from February to May.

This is the most widely distributed of Missouri's early spring flowers.

Plants are 4" to 5" (10 to 13 cm) high at blooming time but grow to almost twice that height later.

Flowers have 5 white or pale pink petals, but the pink impression is often caused by dark pink veins in the petals and the pink anthers. The flowers grow in clusters and open one or two at a time. While there are 5 petals, there are only 2 sepals.

Leaves are deep green, narrow, opposite, and grow from about the middle of the stem.

The rootstock is a thick, rounded corm, edible, tasting like chestnuts when boiled in salt water. Indians used them for food. The green parts of *Claytonia* also are edible and may be fixed as a vegetable.

It is named for John Clayton, one of the first American botanists.

Talinum calycinum [68] Rock Pink, Cherry Bright, Fame Flower

On sandstone and chert outcroppings, glades, south of the Missouri River. **131** Blooms from May to August.

A succulent plant with flower stalks to 12″ (30 cm) high found on rocks, often without apparent soil.

Flowers are borne terminally on delicate stems which branch toward the top. Five cherry-red petals measure to ¾″ (18 mm) across; two small rounded sepals look like a calyx. Stamens vary from 25 to 45. Flowers open around noon or later in the day under clear or cloudy sky and close after a few hours.

Leaves are to 2″ (5 cm) long, fleshy, awl-like, clustered near the base of the stems.

The root is thick and looks like a miniature German Iris rhizome.

Talinum, Greek, means "a green branch," referring to the long-lasting fleshy leaves; *calycinum,* "like a calyx," refers to the sepals.

Talinum parviflorum Cherry Red

On sandstone and chert outcroppings, glades, south of the Missouri River. Blooms from May to August.

Flowers very similar to *T. calycinum,* but smaller and with only 4 to 8 stamens.

Its range and blooming time are similar to the larger-flowered species, but it is much rarer.

PINK FAMILY *Caryophyllaceae*

Dianthus armeria [69] Deptford Pink

In fields, pastures, waste ground, and along roads statewide. Blooms from May to October. Native of Europe.

An extremely slender, stiffly erect annual, grows to 20″ (50 cm) high.

The pink flowers with white dots, in clusters at the tips of the stems, have

5 toothed lobes at the end of a tube. The tube is nearly hidden by long and pointed bracts.

Leaves are very narrow, grass-like, pointed, hairy, opposite.

All four Pinks reported growing in Missouri came from Europe and naturalized in North America. Only *D. armeria* has a wide distribution in our state and may be found in great concentrations in old fields. The other three may not even be found anymore as only isolated occurrences were known.

Dianthus, Greek for "flower of God;" *armeria* is probably from the Celtic *ar,* "near," and *mor,* "sea," referring to the superficial resemblance to the Sea Pink.

132

Silene stellata [24]   Starry Campion, Catchfly

In dry, upland woods and wooded slopes statewide. Blooms from June to September.

Plants from 2 feet to 3 feet (60 to 90 cm) tall.

Flowers grow in a loose terminal spike. They are white, about ¾" (2 cm) across, with 5 united petals, which are fringed, and an inflated, bell-shaped calyx. The stamens are long.

Leaves are in whorls of 4, narrow, lance-shaped, to 3" (8 cm) long.

Silene refers to the god Seilanos who was slippery—the Silene genus has a sticky juice on the stems which traps insects; *stellata,* Latin for "starred."

Silene virginica [64]   Fire Pink

On rocky, wooded slopes of the Ozark region and east-central counties. Blooms from April to June.

Grows to 24" (60 cm) tall with many stems and terminal flowers.

Flowers have strap-like lobes with a single deep notch and are brilliant red or scarlet.

Leaves are opposite, narrow, to 4" (10 cm) long.

Silene refers to the god Seilanos who was slippery. Members of this genus often have sticky stems which catch insects.

Silene antirrhina   Sleepy Catchfly

On roadsides and glades, scattered statewide. Blooms from April to September.

Very small, pink flowers.

Leaves are linear, short, opposite.

The common name Catchfly comes from the sticky bands on stems between leaves which catch small insects.

Saponaria officinalis [74] Soapwort, Bouncing Bet

On gravel and sandbars, waste ground, along roads and railroads statewide. Blooms from June to October. Native of Europe.

Grows on unbranched stalks to about 2 feet (60 cm) high.

Pleasantly spicy fragrant flowers, each about 1″ (25 mm) across, grow in clusters on and toward the top of the stalk. Flower stalks arise from leaf axils. Colors are pink-lilac to white. The 5 petals are slightly notched.

Leaves are 2″ to 3″ (5 to 8 cm) long, opposite, dull green, broadly lance-shaped, have strong parallel veins (3 to 5), and lack stems.

It is called Soapwort because the plant contains a mucilageous juice which forms lather in water.

Saponaria, Latin, means "soap-plant;" *officinalis*, Latin, indicates a medicinal use sometime in the past.

133

WATER LILY FAMILY *Nymphaeaceae*

Nelumbo lutea [46] American Lotus

In oxbow lakes, sloughs, ponds, scattered statewide. Blooms from late June to September.

Fairly still water with a mud bottom is the habitat of *Nelumbo* which often covers large areas.

The light yellow, Water Lily-like flowers are held above the water, growing to 8″ (20 cm) across, and have in their center an elevated receptacle containing the ovaries. As the seeds ripen this receptacle grows to 5″ (13 cm) wide and becomes woody, holding the acorn-like seeds in deep pits.

The leaves are circular, to 2 feet (60 cm) in diameter, attached to a stem at their center. They shed water.

The American Lotus was an important food plant for the Indians. The squaws dug up the starchy roots with their feet. The young shoots were eaten as vegetables and the green seeds taste like chestnuts. When ripe the seeds can be hulled and roasted.

Wildfowl also eat the seeds which are reported to remain viable for many years. Lotus colonies are important nurseries for fish and other aquatic life, as well as shelter for ducks.

Nelumbo is a word of Ceylonese origin for the Hindu lotus; *lutea*, Latin for "yellow."

CUSTARD APPLE FAMILY *Annonaceae*

Asimina triloba [57]   Pawpaw, Missouri Banana

In wooded valleys, along streams, in rich soil statewide. Blooms from
March to May.

An understory tree usually of low height, rarely over 20 feet (6 m) tall,
often growing in dense stands as it sends up suckers from the roots.

The flowers generally appear before or with the leaves. They have 6
petals in two sets of 3-lobed layers (thus *triloba*). The petals are
green at first but turn a deep purple-brown or maroon with age. The
flowers emit a scent resembling fermenting grapes. The color, as well
as the smell, attracts insects which live on decaying matter.

134

The leaves are very large, up to 12″ (30 cm) long and 5″ (13 cm) wide,
elliptical and smooth.

The fruit is oblong, 3″ to 5″ (7 to 13 cm) long, like a small banana. It
contains a delicious custard in which the oval seeds are imbedded.
The fruit is eaten by people as well as opossums, raccoons and squir-
rels. A late frost in spring frequently destroys the fruit crop.

Asimina, a French-Indian name.

CROWFOOT FAMILY *Ranunculaceae*

Anemone canadensis [14]   White Anemone

On river flood plains and low moist situations, primarily along the Missouri and Mississippi Rivers. Blooms from May to July.

The plant grows 12″ to 18″ (30 to 45 cm) high on hairy stems.

Pure white flowers have 5 petal-like sepals with many yellow stamens.
They are carried above the leaves.

Leaves on the stalks are stemless; those emerging from the plant base are
on long stems. All are deeply cut and toothed.

The sight of *A. canadensis* blooming in unbroken carpets on the dikes
near the Mississippi River in northeastern Missouri is one never to be
forgotten.

Anemone, Greek for "windflower."

Anemone caroliniana   Prairie Anemone

On prairies and meadows in southwest Missouri. Blooms from March to
early May.

It has one white flower, tipped with lavender or pink and rose, to a stem.
Basal leaves are deeply divided.

Anemone virginiana [8]   Thimbleweed, Tall Anemone

In rocky, dry, open woods, prairies, statewide except southeast lowlands. Blooms from late April to August.

Plants are to 3½ feet (over 1 m) high, abundant but never in groups, often on wooded hillsides.

Flowers are about 1″ (25 mm) across with off-white, petal-like sepals and a high, dome-like center which give the plant its common name, Thimbleweed.

Leaves are 3-divided with deeply cleft and large-toothed leaflets. The basal leaves on long stalks are similar to those arising from the main stem.

The "thimble"-shaped seed mass remains on the stalk through most of the fall and winter.

Anemone, Greek for "wind-flower."

135

Anemonella thalictroides [2]   Rue Anemone

On open wooded slopes statewide except southeast lowlands and northwest. Blooms from March to June.

An early flowering, delicate plant to 9″ (23 cm) tall.

The flower usually has 5, but sometimes up to 10, petal-like sepals. They are usually white, but may be magenta-pink. An extremely rare double-flowering specimen has been found. The flowers, with many yellowish-green stamens, appear in clusters, but each flower is on an individual stem arising from a common axil.

Leaf-like bracts, 3-lobed and dark olive green, arise from the same axil from which the flowers grow. After flowering, leaf-bearing stems arise from the ground. The true leaves are 3-lobed and look just like the bracts.

Anemonella is one of the longest flowering of the spring flowers. The False Rue Anemone *(Isopyrum)* is very similar in appearance.

Anemonella, Greek with a Latin diminutive ending meaning "little wind-flower;" *thalictroides* because the leaves resemble *Thalictrum,* the Meadow Rue.

Aquilegia canadensis [64]   Columbine

On limestone ledges and rocky slopes in woods statewide except southeast lowlands. Blooms from April to July.

Plants up to 2 feet (60 cm) tall often emerge from nearby perpendicular cliffs.

The flowers, with their 5 long spurs, are unmistakable. The petals are 5 tubes which end in spurs while the 5 sepals are yellow leaflets appended to the petals. The color is yellow grading to scarlet in the spurs.

Leaves are olive green, 3-divided, and deeply lobed.

This is a graceful plant which ranges from the Atlantic to the Pacific Oceans.

Aquilegia, either Latin *aquila* for "eagle," because the spurs resemble claws, or from Latin *aqua,* "water" and *leger,* "to collect," because fluid does collect in the hollow spurs.

Clematis fremontii [7]   Fremont's Leather Flower

On limestone glades of the eastern Ozarks. Blooms in April and May.

136   A showy plant of clump-like growth on open glades. It is the only non-climbing *Clematis* in Missouri.

The white or lavender flower hangs bell-like from stalks up to 2 feet (60 cm) tall.

Leaves are broad, ovate, opposite, with parallel veining, to nearly 5″ (13 cm) long, forming dense foliage. The leaves stay in place through the winter with only the filigree of their veining remaining. These lacy but tough leaves are much esteemed for dried flower arrangements.

C. fremontii is found only in a few counties south and west of St. Louis. Botanists do not agree whether it is a separate species or a subspecies of very similar plants growing in Kansas and Nebraska.

Clematis, Greek name for a climbing plant; *fremontii,* for the explorer and general, John C. Fremont.

Delphinium tricorne [81]   Dwarf Larkspur

In woods, along roads, on ledges and banks of streams statewide. Blooms from April to early June.

This larkspur shows a considerable range of colors, from white or bluish-white to shades of blue to deep violet. Early blooming plants are usually 6″ to 10″ (15 to 25 cm) high, but later grow to 18″ (45 cm). One of the five sepals forms the spur which is nearly 1″ (25 mm) long.

Leaves are divided into finger-like narrow divisions.

Honey bees and bumble bees fertilize Larkspur. The plant is poisonous to cattle.

Delphinium, Greek for "dolphin," referring to the shape of the flower; *tricorne,* Latin, "with 3 horns," is also descriptive of the flower shape.

Delphinium carolinianum [85]   Carolina Larkspur

On glades, prairies, and rocky slopes along and south of the Missouri River. Blooms in May and June.

A showy Larkspur to 3 feet (90 cm) tall with flowers in several colors; sky blue to deep blue, violet-lavender, pink, purple or white. Flowers are large with up-turned spurs which are ¾" (2 cm) long.

Leaves are either 3 or 5 parted into very narrow strap-like lobes.

Delphinium, Greek for "dolphin," describing the shape of the flower.

Delphinium virescens Prairie Larkspur

On prairies and openings in woods in unglaciated western Missouri. Blooms from May to July.

Nearly identical in appearance to *D. carolinianum,* but flowers are white or greenish-white, or tinged only with blue or lilac.

137

Hepatica nobilis [2] *(triloba)* Liverleaf

In rich soils on steep, rocky slopes, absent from western one-third of the state. Blooms in March and April, sometimes again in the fall.

One of the earliest blooming plants, the flowers appear on silky, hairy stems about 6" (15 cm) high before the leaves. The flowers' 5 to 9 petal-like sepals range from milky white to deep lavender-blue, sometimes pink. They are surrounded by last year's leathery, decaying leaves in beautiful shades of wine-red and brown.

The 3-lobed leaves are light green at first but turn to deep olive. They last through summer and part of the winter. Each leaf is supported by a hairy stem.

Hepatica, Latin for "like a liver," probably for the color of the dead leaves, but possibly for the leaf shape; *nobilis,* Latin, "noble."

Hydrastis canadensis [12] Golden Seal

On rich wooded slopes and valleys, absent from northern and southwest counties. Blooms in April and May.

In early spring a hairy stalk grows from 12" to 15" (30 to 38 cm) high bearing two leaves. Each leaf has its own stem arising from a common axil.

Later, from the center of the leaf axil arises one flower stem with a single off-white, rounded flower.

Still later in the season, leaves grow on long stems directly from the roots. Both early and later leaves are divided into 5 to 7 lobes with large teeth.

The fruit is a cluster of deep-red berries which may remain until late fall.

The root is thick, knotted and yellow. Both root and plant have medicinal properties, a characteristic which has made it one of the endangered plants threatened by commercial root diggers, though there are some valleys where hundreds, even thousands, still grow.

Hydrastis refers to *hydro*, Greek for "water," as the plant prefers moist situations.

Isopyrum biternatum [2]   False Rue Anemone

On open wooded slopes and in bottom lands statewide except southeast lowlands. Blooms from March to May.

Plants are 5″ to 8″ (13 to 20 cm) high often forming extensive mats.

Flowers are 5 white petal-like sepals on stems arising from the leaf axils, practically indistinguishable from Anemonella. It flowers in earliest spring, even before Anemonella.

The leaves are divided into either 3 or 9 leaflets. Each leaflet is 3-lobed with lobes which are deeper than those of Anemonella and are pointed.

Isopyrum, Greek name for *Fumaria*, a plant with similar foliage; *biternatum*, Latin for "twice in sets of three," referring to the leaves and leaflets.

Ranunculus hispidus [29]   Hispid Buttercup

Mostly in dry places, ridges, woods, on acid and cherty soils in southeast and south-central Missouri. Blooms from March to early June.

A hairy plant with spreading, but ascending, branches.

Flowers have usually 5 shiny, yellow petals and 5 sepals, often recurved, which are one-half as long as the petals.

Leaves 3 or 5-divided on long petioles, the central leaf section on its own stem, the continuation of the petiole, while the lateral leaf sections attach without stems to the petiole. This feature helps identify the species.

Ranunculus, Latin, "little frog," either because the seeds are supposed to resemble a frog or because many European species are associated with water; *hispidus*, Latin, "densely hairy."

Ranunculus harveyi [29]   Harvey's Buttercup

In acid soils on wooded, rocky slopes and rocky open ground in south and east-central Missouri. Blooms from March to May.

A slender, low and branched plant usually around 12″ (30 cm) high but sometimes to 18″ (45 cm).

Flowers bright yellow, the 4 to 8 petals shiny, as if "buttered," with considerable variation in the size of flowers. Sepals very short and recurved. Many stamens and seed containers (carpels), a characteristic of the Ranunculus Family.

Leaves near the base on long stalks, lobed and kidney-shaped. Upper leaves either 3-lobed or strap-like.

The many seed capsules first form a pointed pyramid and later a rounded fruit-head.

R. harveyi is entirely restricted to the Ozark hills, be they in Missouri, southern Illinois, Arkansas, or northwestern Oklahoma.

Ranunculus, Latin, "little frog," either because the seeds are supposed to resemble a frog or because many European species are associated with water; *harveyi* for Francis Leroy Harvey (1850-1900) who, according to Grey's Manual, was the discoverer of the species.

Ranunculus septentrionalis   Swamp or Marsh Buttercup   139

In moist places along streams or ravines statewide. Blooms from April to June.

Similar to *R. hispidus*, but generally without hair. Plant is much branched with creeping stems.

Flowers are fair sized with shiny yellow petals, usually 5.

Leaves are 3-divided, coarsely toothed, the lateral leaf sections usually on short stems.

Ranunculus fascicularis   Early Buttercup

Near streams and in moist places statewide. Blooms from March to May.
A fairly small plant.

Flowers are yellow and smaller than *R. septentrionalis* or *hispidus*.

Leaves and stems grey-green due to hairiness, 3 to 5-divided, with narrow segments, linear oblong, without teeth.

Ranunculus recurvatus   Hooked Crowfoot

On alluvial mudflats and gravel bars in the Ozarks and a few counties north of the Missouri River. Blooms from May to July.

Yellow flowers are small.

Leaves and stems are hairy. Leaves are broadly kidney-shaped, deeply 3-cleft, on long stems.

Ranunculus abortivus   Small-flowered Crowfoot

Variable habitat, but always moist. Blooms from March to June.
The entire plant is hairy.

Flowers are very small with minute petals.

Basal leaves on long, thick petioles, round and lobed. Leaves on stems sessile and usually divided into 3 narrow, irregular lobes.

Ranunculus micranthus   Rock Crowfoot

On moist or dry uplands or lowlands of central and southern counties. Blooms from March to May.

Very similar to *R. aborvitus* but without hair.

Ten more Ranunculus species are rare or of limited distribution.

Thalictrum revolutum [55]   Waxy Meadow Rue

140

In prairies, open woods, along roads and railroads south of the Missouri River and in northeast counties. Blooms from May to July.

A number of Meadow Rues in Missouri look very much alike. The much-branched stem grows to 5 feet (1.5 m) tall. Both stems and flowers are often light purple, but may also be green.

Flowers, in loose clusters, are each about ¼″ (6 mm) across with 5 petals and many stamens.

Leaves are compound, arising without a common leaf stalk (petiole) from the main stem. Leaflets are often rolled under at the edges with glandular hairs on the under side.

Thalictrum, Greek, is a name used by Pliny and Dioscorides in the 1st century for the Meadow Rue; *revolutum* refers to the leaflet margins which are rolled under.

Thalictrum dioicum   Early Meadow Rue

On rich, north-facing slopes scattered south of the Missouri River. Blooms from early April to May.

Very similar to *T. revolutum* but the compound leaves of the middle and upper part of the stem are attached to the main stem with a long leaf stalk (petiole).

Flowers are yellowish-green, sometimes tinged with purple.

BARBERRY FAMILY *Berberidaceae*

Podophyllum peltatum [4]   May Apple, Mandrake

In low, moist or dry open woods statewide. Blooms from March to May.

A single white flower on a slender stalk emerges from the leaf axil of 2-leafed plants only. It is situated well below the umbrella-like leaves, has 6 to 9 waxy, spreading petals, many stamens, and a green, club-shaped pistil. To about 3″ across (8 cm).

One or two large leaves, held horizontally, spread to 12″ (30 cm) in diameter and to 18″ (45 cm) above the ground. They are palmately lobed and coarsely toothed and arise from a common axil.

The plants often form large colonies.

The fruit, the May Apple, is an egg-sized berry, greenish-yellow when ripe, and has a pleasant taste.

Leaves and roots are poisonous and have medicinal use.

Podophyllum, Greek for "foot-leaf;" *peltatum*, Latin for "shield-shaped."

LAUREL FAMILY *Lauraceae*

Sassafras albidum [30]   Sassafras

In dry, acid soils, borders of woods, prairies, fence rows, in valleys south of the Missouri River and in east-central counties. Blooms in April and May.

Mostly seen as small trees, specimens of more than 2 feet (60 cm) in diameter and 60 feet (18 m) in height exist. It grows in colonies from suckers.

Flowers are in clusters at ends of branches, yellowish-green, each about ¼″ (6 mm) across. Male and female flowers grown on separate trees.

Leaves to 7″ (18 cm) long, pointed, either unlobed or with up to 3 lobes, frequently of uneven sizes, narrowing toward the base. Leaves and twigs are pleasantly aromatic.

The fall color is a rich gold.

Fruits and dark berries in clusters hanging from deep red stalks. They are eaten by birds.

The roots and bark contain an aromatic oil used medicinally and in drinks (root beer).

Sassafras is believed to be the name given to the tree by early French settlers in Florida. It is based on confusion with the plant *Saxifraga—saxum*, Latin for "rock" and *phragein*, Greek for "to break;" *albidum*, Latin for "whitish," referring to the bloom on buds and young branches.

Lindera benzoin [30]   Spice Bush

In low moist woods, along streams, and in bottomlands south of the Missouri River and in east-central counties. Blooms from March to May.

A shrub to 15 feet (4.5 m) high producing masses of greenish-yellow flowers in early spring before the foliage appears.

Spice Bush has male and yellow female flowers on separate shrubs. The male flowers are larger and in showier masses than the female. Flowers are in clusters on short stems along the branches.

The leaves are alternate on petioles, thick, pointed, pear-shaped, much narrowed toward the base, to 12″ (30 cm) long.

141

The fruits are brilliant red drupes about ½″ (12 mm) long.

All parts of the Spice Bush are strongly and pleasantly aromatic.

Lindera is named for Johann Linder (1676-1723), a Swedish botanist; *benzoin,* Arabic or Semitic for "a gum or perfume."

POPPY FAMILY *Papaveraceae*

Sanguinaria canadensis [5]   Bloodroot

On rich wooded slopes and valley bottoms statewide except northwest and southeast bottomlands. Blooms in March and April.

The flower opens before the rolled-up leaf, which envelops the flower stalk, unfurls. As the flower opens 2 sepals fall off and from 8 to 16 snow-white petals descend to a horizontal position to form a flower 1½″ (4 cm) across. Petals are of uneven length and surround the bright yellow stamens. Each flower lasts only one day.

The leaf opens into a many-lobed, dark green, horizontal umbrella, to 8″ (20 cm) across and persists to the middle of summer.

The root is a horizontal, fleshy tuber with a senna-red juice—thus Bloodroot. This juice was used by the Indians for dye.

Sanguinaria, from Latin *sanguis,* "blood."

Stylophorum diphyllum [33]   Celandine Poppy

In rich, low woods and along streams in woods in central and southeast counties. Blooms from April to June.

A much-branched, soft stemmed plant to 18″ (45 cm) tall.

The flowers are rich yellow with 4 rounded petals and many stamens, 2″ (5 cm) across.

Bluish-green leaves, opposite on the stems and basal, are compound. The basal leaves are on long stems. Leaflets are much-lobed, spaced at intervals on the leaf stem, opposite and terminal. The underside of the leaves is silvery grey.

Stems have a dark yellow juice.

It is a prolific seeder which succeeds well in shaded, humus-rich gardens.

Stylophorum, Greek for "style-bearing," referring to the persistent style; *diphyllum,* Greek for "two-leaved," referring to leaves on stems.

FUMITORY FAMILY *Fumariaceae*

Corydalis flavula [32]   Pale Corydalis

In rich woods, along streams, below bluffs in south and central Missouri. Blooms in April and May.

All *Corydalis* species are delicate, low-growing forest dwellers. At times they form spreading mats interspersed with other spring flowers.

Flowers, produced in small groups at the top of the plant, are pale yellow to yellow, with a spur. They are carried on slender stems which support them toward the center of the flower rather than on the end.

The foliage is much dissected, bluish-green, similar to Dutchman's Breeches.

There are six species of *Corydalis* found in Missouri, all very similar in appearance.

Corydalis is Greek for "crested lark," referring to the spur-shaped flowers; *flavula*, Latin for "yellowish."

Dicentra cucullaria [3]   Dutchman's Breeches

143

In rich woods on slopes, below bluffs, along streams statewide except southeast lowlands. Blooms from March to May.

One of our best known wildflowers with a charming descriptive name. The flowers are white, sometimes a faint pink, borne along the top of the stem in a raceme. Each flower is attached at the "crotch" of the "breeches" to a delicate stem. The "breeches," which hang upside down, are, botanically, spurs. *Corydalis,* a member of the same Family, has a similar arrangement.

Leaves are almost fern-like, deeply cut, bluish-green, on separate stems from those bearing flowers.

The root is a scaly, small bulb.

The Bleeding Heart of our garden is a close relative.

Dicentra, Greek for "two-spurred;" *cucullaria,* Latin, means "hooded" as the tips of a pair of petals are joined over the inner part of the flower.

Dicentra canadensis   Squirrel Corn

In moist, rich, low woodlands, scattered in central Missouri. Blooms in April and May.

Not a common plant, it is much like *D. cuccularia* but the spurs are rounded, heartshaped, creamy white.

MUSTARD FAMILY *Brassicaceae (Cruciferae)*

Barbarea vulgaris [33]   Yellow Rocket, Winter Cress

In fields, along roads and railroads statewide. Blooms from April to June. Native of Europe.

A leafy, much-branched plant and common weed, to 2 feet (60 cm) tall. The bright yellow flowers are about ⅓" (8 mm) across, at the end of stems and branches. The 4 petals are typical of the Mustard Family, pointing cross-like in four directions.

Leaves are feather-like, the basal ones on long petioles and those on the stems sessile, sometimes clasping. The terminal sector of each leaf is much larger than the small leaf-sections below them.

Long, 4-sided seed pods follow the flowers and are well formed while the plant is still blooming.

Barbarea, "an herb of St. Barbara;" *vulgaris,* Latin for "common."

Brassica nigra [33]   Black Mustard

144

In fields, waste ground, along roads, scattered statewide. Blooms from April to November.

A coarse, tall weed to 5 feet (1.5 m) high.

Fragrant, yellow flowers begin to open in early April on top of the stalks, followed immediately by long, slender seed pods. The flowers are small and the petals form a cross, as do all flowers of the Family *Brassicaceae* which was formerly called *Cruciferae* (Latin, "cross-bearer").

Leaves are fleshy, irregularly lobed, reminiscent of the closely related cabbages.

Other Mustards, all escaped from cultivation and all coming from Eurasia, have great variety of leaf shapes. One, *B. rapa,* Field Mustard, has large leaves somewhat like a cauliflower.

Brassica, the classical Latin name for cabbage; *nigra,* Latin for "black," referring to the seeds.

Cardamine bulbosa [5]   Spring Cress

In wet woods, springs and spring branches in south Missouri and some east-central counties north of the Missouri River. Blooms from March to June.

A white-flowered member of the Mustard Family, to 12" (30 cm) tall.

The lower leaves are paddle-shaped, the upper ones triangular, pointed, with large, fleshy teeth.

The base of the stem has been used as a substitute for horse-radish. The names of this species may be confusing. Though named *bulbosa,* the root is not a bulb. The common name, Spring Cress, should not be confused with Water Cress, *Nasturtium officinale.*

Cardamine is the Greek name for a Cress.

Cardamine parviflora   Small-flowered Bitter Cress

On uplands, rocky woods, ridges, scattered statewide. Blooms from March to July.

Quite variable in size.
Feather-like leaves with linear-oblong sections.
Seedpods long.

Cardamine pensylvanica   Bitter Cress

In moist places, scattered in central and southern counties. Blooms from
    March to July.
Flowers and leaves similar to *C. parviflora* but larger.

Dentaria laciniata [3]   Toothwort

In rich woods, slopes or valleys statewide except southeast lowlands.
    Blooms from March to May.

145

One of the earliest flowers of spring. The 4 petals are in cross position,
    slightly upturned, usually white but sometimes pale lavender. Flowers
    are borne above the leaves, along and toward the top of the stem.
Leaves are in a whorl of 3, attached midway on the plant stem. They are
    divided into 3 segments which are pointed and deeply toothed, giving
    a 5-lobed appearance.
The root is a small tuber which has a radish-like flavor and can be eaten
    in salads.
Dentaria, Latin *dens* for "tooth." The reference may be to the slightly
    closed flowers, the toothed leaves, or the roots of certain species. The
    species name, *laciniata*, is Latin for "torn," describing the leaves.

Erysimum capitatum [36]   Western Wall-flower

On limestone bluffs, rocky open ground, scattered in central Missouri river
    valleys. Blooms from May to July.
A showy plant to 2 feet (60 cm) high.
The 4-petalled flowers are ⅝" (15 mm) across in a bright orange or
    orange-yellow color. The perfume of the flowers is outstanding and
    very much reminiscent of *Cheiranthus*, a close relation grown in nearly
    every garden of northern Europe for its perfume.
Leaves are broadly toothed, narrow, borne alternately along the stems.
The few other *Erysimum* species in Missouri are much less conspicuous.
    None has wide distribution.
Erysimum, Greek, ancient name of Hedge Mustard; *capitatum*, Latin,
    means "headed."

Lepidium campestre [6]   Field Cress, Cow Cress, Pepper
Grass

In fields, waste ground, along roads and railroads statewide. Blooms from
    April to June. Native of Europe.

Usually 10″ to 18″ (25 to 45 cm) tall, but even taller in rich soil. It is frequently found in large colonies. The stem is hairy and appears grey-green. It arises straight from basal leaves.

The flowers are carried in clusters on branches near the top. They are tiny, white, with the 4 petals characteristic of the Mustard Family.

Leaves along the stalk are arrow-shaped, broadly toothed, and without stems. The basal leaves look like small Dandelion leaves with rounded ends.

The seeds, in almost round pods on widely spreading stalks, give the Pepper Grass an ornamental, candelabra-like look.

Lepidium, Greek for "small scale," referring to the thin seed capsules; *campestre,* Latin, "of the fields."

146

Lepidium virginicum   Pepper Grass

In open places, roadsides statewide. Blooms from February to November.

Much branched. Lower leaves spoon-shaped; upper leaves oblong-linear. Both are sharply toothed, sessile (without stems), but do not clasp.

Pepper Grass is a name given to many species of the Mustard Family.

Nasturtium officinale [8]   Water Cress

In and around springs and spring branches in southern and central Missouri. Blooms from April to October.

Water Cress is usually found standing in water, rising in much-branched, bushy plants to 8″ or 10″ (20 to 25 cm).

It has masses of minute, 4-petalled, white or lightly lavender-tinted flowers growing at the ends of the branches.

Leaves are dissected with a rounded blade at the end and several opposite, rounded lobes at intervals along the leaf axis.

Water Cress has a sharp flavor and is used in salads or as a dressing. **With our condition of general stream pollution, care must be taken that the plants used for eating come from an uncontaminated water source as the danger of typhoid infection exists.** Water Cress is also frequently host to masses of aphids.

Nasturtium, Latin, means "nose twister," probably for the sharp, mustard-like taste; *officinale,* Latin, indicates a medicinal use sometime in the past.

SAXIFRAGE FAMILY *Saxifragaceae*

Hydrangea arborescens [21]   Wild Hydrangea

On wooded slopes, rock outcroppings near streams, and along streams in south and southeast Missouri. Blooms from May to July.

A shrub to 6 feet (2 m) tall, rarely higher, with light brown, brittle branches. The presence of Hydrangea is always an indicator of available moisture.

Flowers are displayed in dense, flat clusters to 5" (13 cm) across, the central ones minute with 4 or 5 lobes from which the stamens protrude. These are fertile. Usually, but not always, there are at the periphery of the cluster a few large sterile white flowers which show 3 or 4 lobes, membrane-like parts of the floral envelope (calyx) and have neither stamens nor pistil—but serve to attract insects for pollination.

Leaves on petioles, opposite, from 3" to 6" (8 to 15 cm) long, broad oval, much toothed, green above while the underside may be green or pale.

Fruit is a tiny capsule, wider than high.

Hydrangea, Greek, "water" and "vessel," referring to the liking of the genus for moisture and the artistic shape of the seed vessel; *arborescens,* Latin, "shrubby."

The Hydrangeas of our gardens have been developed by selection of plants with the most sterile flowers.

147

Ribes missouriense [7]   Wild or Missouri Gooseberry

In open woods, borders of woods, valleys, upland or lowland, statewide except southeast lowlands. Blooms in April and May.

Shrubs, generally around 4 feet (1.2 m) high, with wide spreading branches. Spines to ⅝" (16 mm) long, either solitary or 2 or 3 together at the joints where leaves and flowers are borne. Few prickles on the stems.

Flowers with a pleasant scent hang drooping from long flower stalks and are white or greenish, to ¾" (18 mm) long. The flowers are unusual with 5 tightly recurved sepals enclosing and almost hiding the bell-shaped, 5-lobed corolla. From this chalice protrude 5 converging stamens and the pistil.

Leaves on long petioles, palmately veined, with from 3 to 5 lobes and prominent teeth, about 3" (8 cm) long.

The fruit, which may mature from June to September, is a pulpy berry, purple or brown, tipped by the remains of the floral envelope (calyx) and roughly ½" (13 mm) in size.

There are two other *Ribes* species in Missouri, but both have very limited distribution.

Ribes, a word of Arabic origin, meaning "berry with an acid juice."

Saxifraga virginiensis [1]   Early Saxifrage

On wooded ledges and bluffs, rocky glades, usually in acid soils, in the

Ozark Region and east-central north to St. Louis. Blooms from February to June.

Starts blooming on a hairy flower stalk 4″ to 6″ (10 to 15 cm) high, but as it continues to bloom it may reach 12″ (30 cm).

Flowers, at first, in a tight, rounded platform, spread out later as the inflorescence branches out. Flowers have 5 petals, about ¼″ (6 mm) across, and 10 stamens.

Leaves form a basal rosette, are fleshy, egg-shaped, narrowing toward the base, with scalloped margins.

Saxifrages are primarily mountain flowers.

148 *Saxifraga*, from *saxum*, Latin for "rock," and *phragein*, Greek, "to break," referring to the reputed ability to remedy kidney and bladder stones, or from their normal occurrence on rocks.

Saxifraga pensylvanica   Swamp Saxifrage

Demands shade and moisture, on and below sandstone bluffs in a few counties around St. Louis. Blooms from April to June.

This plant has been officially declared a rare and endangered species, but it is abundant where it grows.

Massed, tiny green flowers grow on long, leafless flower stems (scapes).

Leaves are basal, large, to 12″ (30 cm) long, oblong, slightly scalloped.

ROSE FAMILY *Rosaceae*

Amelanchier arborea [4] *(canadensis)*   Shadbush, Service Berry

In open woods and on bluffs statewide. Blooms from March to May.

A shrub, often much branched, or a small to medium size tree.

Flowers are a showy white, in clusters, with strap-shaped petals with a drooping appearance. Blooms before leaves emerge.

Leaves are ovate, finely toothed, 2″ to 4″ (5 to 10 cm) long.

Bark is light grey, smooth on young specimens, becoming scaly and forming ridges with age.

Fruit is a red to purple, sweet berry, eaten by people and many species of wildlife.

The name Shadbush refers to the shad which swim up the eastern rivers to spawn at the time when Shadbush is in bloom.

Amelanchier is the name given by the people of the Savoy, in France, to a local species of Service Berry; *arborea*, Latin for "tree forming."

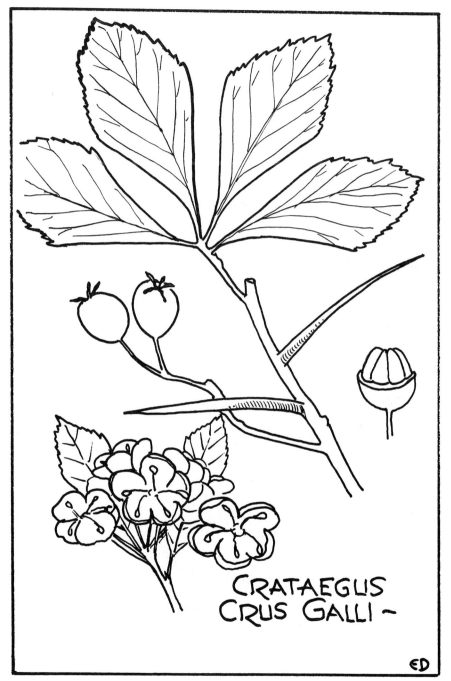

CRATAEGUS
CRUS GALLI ~

ED

HAWTHORN LEAVES

150

ED

Aruncus dioicus [17]   Goat's Beard

In moist woods, along bluffs in central, southern, and eastern counties. Blooms from May to July.

A tall, showy plant, 4 to 5 feet (1.2 to 1.5 m) tall.

Masses of tiny, creamy-white flowers with 5 oval petals grow in plume-like clusters.

The leaves are compound, much divided and toothed. The lower leaflets have stems, the upper ones do not.

It can be readily grown from seeds in shaded places in the garden, but must have humus-rich soil.

This is one of several Missouri wildflowers with the common name Goat's Beard.

Aruncus, classical Latin name for Goat's Beard; *dioicus*, for dioecious, meaning male and female flowers are on separate plants.

151

Crataegus spp [11]   Hawthorn, Red Haw

In old fields, roadsides, varied habitats. Some species grows in every part of Missouri. Blooms in April and May.

The flower of the Hawthorn is the state flower of Missouri. There are 50 distinct species recognized in our state, but only a few have wide distribution.

All have the typical 5-petal flowers which we associate with cultivated fruit trees and are either white or pink.

Leaves are alternate, either egg-shaped or sharply toothed and cut.

Many species have thorns, but not all.

The fruit is apple-like, but usually less than ½″ (12 mm) in diameter. It is a favorite food of many wild birds, including wood ducks, pheasants and grouse.

Crataegus, old Greek for "flowering thorn."

Crataegus crus-galli   Cockspur Thorn

In thickets, borders of woods, roadsides, statewide except southeast lowlands. Blooms in May and June.

Flowers are white.

Leaves are shiny, slightly toothed, ovate, tapering at the base.

There are eight recognized varieties of this small tree.

Crataegus mollis   Summer Haw

In moist places and bottomlands, missing from parts of the Ozarks. Blooms in April.

Flowers are white.
Leaves are finely toothed, broad at base, incised.

Fragaria virginiana [11]   Wild Strawberry

On open slopes, prairies, borders of woods, varied habitats statewide.
Blooms in April and May.
Low, ground-hugging plants.
Flowers are arranged in clusters, each with 5 petals and many stamens,
characteristics of the Rose Family.
Leaves are 3-divided on hairy stems. Leaflets are egg-shaped and toothed.
Strawberries spread through "runners," shoots emerging from the base of
older plants which take root some distance from the parent plant to
form a new plant.
The fruit is a berry esteemed by Man and beast. The taste of Wild Straw-
berries is superior to those grown under cultivation.
Fragaria, Latin from *fragare*, "to have a scent," from the delicious aroma
of the berries, the classical Latin name of the Strawberry.

Geum canadense [19]   White Avens

Rich or rocky woods, valleys, along streams statewide. Blooms from May
to October.
Branched, from 1½ to 2½ feet (45 to 75 cm) tall, finely hairy, especially in
the upper parts.
Flowers white, about ½" (12 mm) wide, with 5 petals interspersed by 5
green sepals of almost equal length. Many stamens.
Leaves usually 3-lobed, the lobes of the lower ones rounded, the upper
ones pointed, prominently toothed. Small leaf-like stipules at points
of branching.
Fruit is a mass of seed receptacles with bristles—burr-like.
Geum is the classical name of one European member of this genus.

Geum vernum   Spring or Early Water Avens

In moist places, low woods along streams, thickets, statewide. Blooms from
April to June.
Small, yellow flowers with many petals.
Leaves rounded, wavy, and toothed.

Gillenia stipulata [19]   Indian Physic, American Ipecac

Dry, rocky, usually acid uplands of central and southern Missouri. Blooms
from May to July.

Gillenia is a tall, leafy plant growing 3 feet (90 cm) high. It sometimes
covers entire hillsides in the Ozark Mountains.

Flowers have 5 showy, pointed petals which are bent backwards. Their
color is either white or light pink.

Leaves are 3-divided, deeply cut with large teeth which are also toothed.
Each leaf is on a very short leafstalk which is flanked by two leaf-like
bracts, called stipules. The stipules are so large and look so much like
the leaves that the leaves appear to be 5-divided. This is the source
of the name *stipulata*.

Indian Physic and Ipecac indicate that American Indians used the plant
for internal cleansing, which seems to be a wide-spread ceremonial requirement for many tribes. Ipecac is an emetic derived from certain **153**
dried roots.

Gillenia is for A. Gille, a German physician and botanist.

Physocarpus opulifolius [16]   Ninebark

In moist places, along streams, below bluffs except in northwest and
north-central counties. Blooms in May and June.

A shrub from 3 feet to 10 feet (.9 to 3 m) high with many recurving
branches.

Flowers are in large clusters, each flower with the 5 rounded white petals
and many stamens typical of the Rose Family.

Leaves are rounded to ovate, more or less 3-lobed, with coarse, blunt
teeth. Some leaves are pointed, some not.

Fruit is in inflated, paper-like pods, usually 3 in a group.

The bark splits and peels into many paper-thin layers—thus Ninebark.

Physocarpus, Greek for "inflated fruit;" *opulifolius*, Latin, "with the leaf
of *(Viburnum) opulus*," the High-bush Cranberry.

Potentilla simplex [35]   Cinquefoil, Five-finger

In open woods, prairies, fields, along roads and railroads statewide. Blooms
from April to June.

Many trailing stems rise up at blooming time.

Flowers with 5 bright yellow petals arise on stems emerging from leaf
axils which have thickened nodes.

Leaves are divided into what looks like 5, but are actually 3, leaflets.
Leaflets are sharply toothed.

Potentilla, Latin for "little potent one," referring to the medicinal use
of some of the many members of this tribe; *simplex*, Latin for "simple"
or "unbranched."

The common name, Cinquefoil, is French for "five leaves."

Potentilla recta [40]   Rough-fruited Cinquefoil

In fields, pastures, roadsides, waste ground statewide. Blooms from May
to August. Native of Europe.

A stout, leafy, quite hairy, much branched perennial to 2 feet (60 cm) tall,
which often covers considerable ground.

Flowers with 5 slightly notched petals which are much larger than the
lobes of the calyx (flower envelope). Flowers are light yellow to
cream, have about 30 stamens, and are ¾" (20 mm) across, in flat clusters.

Leaves compound with 5 to 7 leaflets which are coarsely toothed and
emerge from a common base. Basal leaves on long stalks.

This is a showy immigrant which is not welcome in grazing areas because
the plant is shunned by animals.

Potentilla, Latin for "little potent one," referring to the medicinal use of
some of the many members of this tribe; *recta,* Latin, "upright," the
plant's growth habit.

154

Potentilla norvegica   Rough Cinquefoil

In fields, waste places, roadsides statewide. Blooms from May to October.

Flowers are deep yellow, ½" (12 mm) across, terminal, single when young
but in groups when mature.

Leaves are 3-divided (trifoliate) with coarse teeth.

Prunus americana [6]   Wild Plum

In woodlands, pastures, fence rows statewide. Blooms in April and May.

The largest of many Wild Plum species in Missouri, it is a small tree or
shrub-like with many shoots.

Flowers are white, with 5 petals and many stamens, about 1" (25 mm)
across, and clustered close to branches.

Leaves are alternate, oval, long pointed and finely toothed.

The fruit is a red ball, about 1" (25 mm) in diameter, sweet when fully
ripe, and excellent for marmalades and jellies.

Prunus is the classical Latin name for Plum. Botanically, *Prunus* includes
the Plums, Cherries, Almonds, and Apricots.

Prunus serotina [6]   Black Cherry, Rum Cherry

In low and upland woods, along streams statewide. Blooms in April and
May.

A very valuable tree, 50 to 60 feet (15 to 18 m) high, but occasionally
even taller.

White flowers are clustered on 4" to 6" (10 to 15 cm) long racemes, either erect or nodding. Individual flowers about ¼″ (6 mm) across, with 5 petals.

Leaves are alternate, narrowly oblong with a short point, finely toothed.

Fruit is a small cherry, about the size of a pea, red at first and later turning black. Black Cherry is a star attraction as food for song and game birds.

The beautiful, strong wood resembles mahogany. Principal uses are for furniture, wood turning, and many specialties.

Prunus, classical Latin name for Plum; *serotina,* Latin for "late," because other *Prunus* species bloom earlier.

Pyrus ioensis [63] *(Malus)*   Wild Crab

In open woods, borders of woods and pastures, along streams statewide.   **155**
Blooms in April and May.

Grows from 20 to 30 feet (6 to 9 m) high and can attain a trunk diameter of 18″ (45 cm).

Flowers are in clusters of 3 to 6 along the branches. They have 5 petals and the color may be deep rose-pink, pale pink, or white.

Leaves are alternate, egg-shaped to oblong, irregularly and coarsely toothed.

Branches are tortuous, with many thorn-like, short spurs. Leaves and flowers arise from the sides of these spurs.

Fruit is round, 1″ to 1½″ (25 to 40 mm) in diameter, greenish-yellow, fragrant, but greasy tasting, not good to eat.

Pyrus is the classical Greek name for the "pear tree;" *ioensis,* "from Iowa."

Rosa setigera [66]   Prairie Rose, Climbing Rose

In moist rocky fields, along streams, in fencerows statewide. Blooms from late May to July.

This common Rose may either climb or form sprawling thickets from arching stems.

Flowers may be pink or rose, rarely white, and have 5 petals and many stamens, to 3″ (8 cm) across, with a magnificent perfume.

Leaves on old stems (or canes) 3-divided; on young shoots often 5-divided. Leaflets are toothed.

Rosa, classical Latin name for Rose; *setigera,* Latin, "bristle-bearing."

Of 15 Rose species reported in Missouri, only three have a general distribution.

Rosa carolina   Pasture Rose

In moist places, pastures, fence rows statewide. Blooms in May and June.

Low growing plants with prickly stems.

Flower color is variable pale to deep rose, rarely white.

Leaves 3 to 7-divided.
Height, shape of leaflets, and thorniness are variable.

Rosa multiflora   Multiflora or Japanese Rose

Introduced, often escaped from fencerows, statewide. Blooms in May and
 June. Native of Asia.
Canes to 8 feet (2.5 m) long, plants spread over 12 feet (3.6 m).
Flowers white, in clusters, with 5 petals.
The red fruit—the rose hips—are esteemed by birds, as is the impenetrable
 jungle of canes as nesting and escape cover by birds and animals.

156

Rubus flagellaris [11]   Dewberry

In prairies, fields, along roads and railroads statewide. Blooms from April
 to June.
The Dewberry is a trailing thorny briar.
Flowers are white, about ¾″ (18 mm) across, with 5 petals.
Leaves are 3 or 5-divided, broadly ovate, toothed.
Dewberries are large, shiny black, and of course, edible. They are an
 important wildlife food.
The genus *Rubus* includes the Blackberries and Raspberries. They all have
 very similar flowers, form shrubs or trail, and invade land that has
 been disturbed. We have 16 species of *Rubus* in Missouri, but identi-
 fying them is a job for experts.
Rubus, from Latin *ruber*, "red;" *flagellaris*, Latin, "whip-like."

PEA FAMILY *Fabaceae (Leguminosae)*

Amorpha canescens [86]   Lead Plant

In prairies, glades, rocky open woods, statewide except southeast lowlands.
 Blooms from May to August.
A shrub to 3 feet (90 cm) tall.
Flowers are massed on spikes at the end of stems and are purple with
 yellow stamens protruding. Though a member of the Pea Family, the
 flowers have only one petal with neither wings or keel.
The compound leaves are divided into as many as 35 small, rounded leaf-
 lets. Leaves are grey and quite hairy.
It is an important plant for browsing animals.
It is assumed that the name Lead Plant comes from the grey appearance.
Amorpha, Greek meaning "without shape" or "deformed," referring to the
 simplified flower; *canescens*, Latin for "grey hair."

Astragalus mexicanus [31]   Ground Plum, Milk Vetch, Buffalo Pea

In rocky open woods, embankments, glades, prairies along and south of the Missouri River. Blooms from March to May.

Branched, bushy plants about 20″ (50 cm) high.

The flowers, nearly 1″ (25 mm) across, are cream colored with lilac-blue at the tip of the pointed keel petal.

The long leaves are pinnately divided into many smooth leaflets, up to 33 per leaf.

The fruit, a long pod, is edible in the unripe state.

Astragalus, Greek name for a member of the Pea Family.

157

Astragalus canadensis   Rattle Weed

In open lowlands or upland woods statewide. Blooms from May to August.

A tall, upright plant to 4 feet (1.2 m).

Long inflorescences with greenish-yellow flowers.

Compound leaves with many leaflets which are opposite and get shorter toward the tip of the leaf stem.

Baptisia leucantha [21]   White Wild Indigo

In prairies, glades, along streams statewide. Blooms from May to July.

A much-branched plant which prefers wet soil; at its best along Ozark streams. Plant sometimes over 5 feet (1.5 m) tall.

Pure white flowers grow in erect or curved racemes.

The leaves are divided into 3 leaflets. Plant stems have a grayish-white covering.

It is possible that *B. leucantha* is poisonous.

Baptisia, Greek, "to dye," as certain species provide coloring substances; *leucantha*, Greek, "white-flowered."

Baptisia leucophaea [34]   Long-bracted Wild Indigo

In rocky, dry, open woods, prairies, mostly in acid soils statewide except southeast lowlands. Blooms from April to June.

Low, bush-like plants to 12″ (30 cm) high. The earliest blooming *Baptisia*.

The showy, cream-colored flowers are borne on long, drooping or horizontal branches called racemes. The individual flowers are similar to those of peas or beans.

Leaf and flower stems have prominent leaf-like bracts.

Foliage is dark green, each leaf divided into 3 smooth-edged leaflets to 2″ (5 cm) long.

Seeds are in long, pointed pods.

The common name Indigo refers to the use of the plant as a dye, though
of poor quality.

Baptisia, Greek, "to dye;" *leucophaea*, Greek, "cream-colored."

Baptisia australis   Blue False Indigo

On limestone glades and prairies of south and east-central Missouri.
Blooms from early May to June.

Plants spreading, about 18″ (45 cm) tall but sometimes much taller.

Blue to violet flowers borne in racemes.

Leaves on short petioles, trifoliate.

The flowers have been used as a poor substitute for indigo.

158

Cassia marilandica [50]   Wild Senna

In open, rocky woods, base of slopes, wet meadows statewide. Blooms in
July and August.

A tall plant, from 3 to 8 feet (.9 to 2.4 m) high, which prefers wet situations. The stem is usually upright, unbranched.

The small, orange-yellow flowers are in clusters along the stem. They are
about ½″ (12 mm) in diameter with 5 spreading petals, two larger
than the others.

Leaves, divided into 10 to 20 oval and pointed leaflets, grow along the
stem and between the flower clusters.

Seed pods to 4″ (10 cm) long.

Senna leaves have been used in medicine as a cathartic.

Cassia is an ancient Greek name for the Cassia-bark Tree which Linnaeus
applied to this genus.

Cassia fasciculata [46]   Partridge Pea

On prairies, glades, along roads and railroads statewide. Blooms from June
to October.

This member of the Pea family is a familiar sight along roadsides where
it grows to 2 feet (60 cm) tall.

The yellow flowers are 1½″ (4 cm) across, often with a touch of red-purple
spots at the base. The flowers emerge along the stems from the leaf
axils.

**Leaves pinnate with 6 to 18 pairs of narrow, short, linear leaflets, which
fold together when touched.**

The pea-pod shaped seed pod grows to 2½″ (7 cm) long. Seeds are eaten
by quail and other birds.

Cassia is an ancient Greek name; *fasciculata*, Latin, "in bunches."

Cassia nictitans   Sensitive Pea

On acid soils of open woods south of the Missouri River. Blooms from
  July to September.
Low, spreading, to 12″ (30 cm) tall.
Flowers yellow, very small, along the stems.
Leaflets are like other *Cassias* but very small.

Cercis canadensis [60]   Redbud, Judas Tree

In open woods, glades statewide. Blooms from late March to early May.
Usually a small understory tree, but sometimes, as an ornamental, it
  reaches a diameter of 12″ (30 cm) or more.
Purple-red to pink-lavender flowers, in the typical shape of pea or bean
  flowers, grow all along the stems.
A white form, found only once in the wild, is now being cultivated.
The heart-shaped leaves are large and change their position during the
  hot hours of the day from horizontal to a vertical position to minimize
  evaporation.
The seed pods, 2″ to 3″ (5 to 8 cm) long, are produced in great masses.
Redbuds are much weakened in transplanting and often fall victim to
  borers.
Judas Tree comes from a legend that Judas hanged himself from a tree
  of this genus.
Cercis is the name of the Oriental Judas Tree.

159

Clitoria mariana [71]   Butterfly Pea

In acid soils along streams and rich bottomlands in central and southern
  Missouri. Blooms from May to September.
A low growing or trailing plant which is not very common and a thrill to
  find. It trails but does not climb.
The pea-like flowers are not only very large, to 2″ (5 cm) across, but also
  beautifully colored pale blue-lilac with darker purple pencilling. They
  arise from leaf axils. At least one author states that *Clitoria* also develops very small, bud-like flowers late in the season which also produce viable seeds.
The seed pod is about 2″ (5 cm) long.
Clitoria, a reference to the resemblance of the flower shape to human
  anatomy; *mariana*, from Maryland.

Coronilla varia [69]   Crown Vetch

In roadways, fields, waste places. Massively planted along highways statewide. Blooms from May to August. Native of Europe, Asia, Africa.

A creeping groundcover about 12″ (30 cm) high.

Flowers are massed in umbels, like a "crown." Individual flowers, typical of the Pea Family, are pink and white, sometimes all white.

Leaves are pinnate with small, opposite, oblong leaflets.

Crown Vetch has been widely planted along roads and highways in the northern ⅔ of Missouri.

Coronilla, Latin, "little crown;" *varia*, Latin for "diverse," referring to the variable coloring of the flowers.

Coronilla resembles a Vetch but does not belong to the genus *Vicia*—Vetch.

160 *Desmodium canescens* [77] Tick-trefoil, Beggar's Lice

In dry, open woods, valleys, scattered statewide. Blooms from July to September.

A tall plant, 3 to 4 feet (.9 to 1.2 m) high. Other *Desmodium* species are trailing plants.

D. canescens has panicles of small but showy rose-purple flowers. All Desmodiums have the typical pea-shaped flowers, usually in rose-purple or shades of magenta-pink. A few are white.

Leaves are 3-divided, egg-shaped and pointed.

Seeds are in pods which are segmented for each seed, each segment a nearly triangular shape. The number of seeds and shape of pod varies with the species.

The seed pods are hairy and stick to clothing, an aggravating characteristic responsible for the common name, Beggar's Lice.

Desmodium is an important browse plant for deer, and the seeds are eaten by many birds.

Desmodium, Greek meaning "a band or chain," descriptive of the seed pods; *canescens*, Latin, "grey-downy."

There are 18 Tick-trefoil species in Missouri. Identification of the individual species is quite difficult for the amateur and often depends on analysis of the seed structure.

Lathyrus latifolius [65] Everlasting Pea, Perennial Pea

In fencerows, along roads and railroads, in thickets scattered statewide. Blooms from May to September. Native of Europe.

A strong climber, often covering large areas. The stems are broadly winged with wings on two sides.

Flowers are clustered inflorescences with up to 10 flowers, each about 1″ (25 mm) long, in a variety of colors including rose-purple, deep rose. pink, and white. They have a large standard and a relatively small keel, and they have no scent.

Leaves are 3-divided: a narrow winged basal portion ends in tendrils; two lance-shaped leaflets branch from the basal winged section symmetrically.

Lathyrus, a Greek name for some Legume; *latifolius,* Latin for "broad-leaved."

Lespedeza violacea [76]   Bush Clover

161

In rocky, dry upland woods, prairies, clearings statewide except in southeast lowlands. Blooms from July to September.

Found in the Ozarks as either an upright plant growing to 2½ feet (75 cm) tall or spreading. When upright it appears bush-like with many spreading branches from the base, thus Bush Clover.

Light magenta flowers, to ⅓″ (8 mm) across, are borne in clusters on slender, spreading stalks. They have the typical pea flower shape.

Leaves are 3-divided, the leaflets oval with rounded tops, ½″ to 2″ (12 mm to 5 cm) long and ¾″ (2 cm) wide.

Seeds, in pods, are eaten by quail, turkey, and other birds.

Lespedeza is named for a Spanish governor of Florida, Manuel de Lespedeza.

There are 15 species of *Lespedeza* found in Missouri, many difficult for the layman to identify. Some have white flowers, others are yellowish or violet. All have the 3-divided leaves of the Pea Family.

Lespedeza virginica [68]   Bush Clover

In dry, open woods, prairies, margins of streams, along roads and railroads statewide except extreme northwest. Blooms from late May to September.

Plants to 3 feet (90 cm) high, unbranched, with many leaves. The stalks usually curve under their own weight.

Flowers arise from the leaf axils and cover the upper section of the plant stalk. They are pea-flower shaped, small and pink.

Leaves are 3-divided into narrow, linear leaflets only ¼″ (6 mm) or less wide and 2¼″ (6 cm) long.

The seeds, carried in pods, are eaten by many birds.

Lespedeza is named for Manuel de Lespedez, a Spanish governor of Florida, who helped the French botanist Michaux in the late 18th century.

Lotus corniculatus [43]   Bird's-foot Trefoil

In fields, along roads, waste ground, scattered where originally planted.
Blooms from May to September. Native of Europe.

A perennial legume with many branches which, though they lie on the
ground, have ascending ends (decumbent).

Flowers are a rich golden yellow, each ½″ (12 mm) long, and carried
terminally in umbels.

Leaves are compound with 5 leaflets, 3 at the end of the leafstalk and 2
at the base. The base leaflets are referred to as stipules by some authors. The shape of the leaflets, generally oblong, varies.

162   Fruit is contained in many slender awl- or horn-shaped pods about 1″
(25 mm) long. They stand upright in groups on the flowering stalks.

The species comes from Europe, but has a wide distribution in all other
continents. The plant, being able to take care of itself even in poor
and dry soils, has been planted widely in the northern ⅔ of the state.
As it grows low, it does not need mowing. Bird's-foot Trefoil may
spread into southern Missouri, but it is not presently common there.
It has also been experimented with widely as a pasture plant.

Lotus, in antiquity a much used name for a number of quite different
genera, was selected by Linnaeus exclusively for this genus of clovers;
corniculatus, Latin, "little horned," describes the seed pods.

Melilotus officinalis [36]   Yellow Sweet Clover, Yellow Melilot

In fields, waste places, along roads and railroads statewide. Blooms from
May to October. Native of Europe and Asia.

Tall, rigidly branched plants to 6 feet (1.8 m) high.

The tiny, light yellow flowers grow in spikes to 4″ (10 cm) long. They are
pea-flower shaped and have a strongly perfumed fragrance. Blooms are
produced over a long period.

Leaves are 3-divided with stipules at their base. The leaflets, narrow to
oval, rounded at the top, are finely toothed.

Highly drought resistant, it has been planted for hay, pasture, and green
manuring.

Melilotus, Greek for "honey-lotus;" *officinalis* means the plant has had
medicinal application.

Melilotus albus   White Sweet Clover

All information is identical to *M. officinalis* except that flowers are white.

Petalostemon purpureum [73]   Purple Prairie Clover

On prairies, open rocky glades and woods, along railroads statewide except southeast lowlands. Blooms from June to September.

Grows to 3 feet (90 cm) tall.

The many flowers are in cylindrical spikes resembling a thimble with a plug inserted. The buds are covered with silvery hair. The tiny, rose-magenta or rose-purple flowers open in a circle, beginning at the bottom of the spike and moving upward as the season advances.

Leaves are 3 or 5-divided with a terminal leaflet and 1 or 2 sets of linear leaflets spreading from the midrib. Each leaf is accompanied by extremely narrow bracts.

Petalostemon, Greek for "petal and stamen," alluding to the unusual union of these floral parts in this genus.

163

Petalostemon candidum   White Prairie Clover

All information is identical to *P. purpureum* except that flowers are white.

Psoralea onobrychis [88]   French Grass

On wooded slopes, low open ground, river banks, in valleys of eastern Missouri. Blooms from May to September.

A leafy, much-branched plant to 2½ feet (75 cm) tall.

Small, pale blue or purple pea-type flowers grow in loose, upright spikes which arise on long stems from the leaf axils.

Leaves are alternate, 3-divided, with the middle leaflet on a long stalk and the side leaflets on short stems. Leaflets are smooth, lance-shaped to ovate, long-pointed.

Psoralea, Greek for "scurfy" from the dots which cover leaves and stems; *onobrychis* indicates the plant looks like an *Onobrychis*, another member of the Pea Family.

Psoralea psoralioides   Sampson's Snakeroot

On acid soils in openings in woods and open situations south of the Missouri River. Blooms from May to July.

Its appearance similar to *P. onobrychis*, but flower clusters on very long stalks and trifoliate leaves with narrow leaflets on very short petiole. Leaflets to 3" (8 cm) long.

Psoralea tenuiflora   Scurfy Pea, Few-flowered Psoralea

On limestone soils of glades and prairies, open woods, absent from southern counties. Blooms from May to September.

Taller than other described *Psoraleas*, to 4 feet (1.2 m).

Flowers smallish, purplish, spaced apart.

Leaves 3-divided on short stems with short leaflets, not quite 1" (25 mm) long.

Psoralea esculenta   Prairie Turnip, Indian Breadroot, Wild Potato

On rocky prairies, glades, open slopes, scattered south of the Missouri River. Blooms from April to July.

A very hairy plant, not over 18″ (45 cm) high.

Flowers dull purple in dense clusters.

Leaves 5-divided, palmate.

The roots were eaten by Indians and early settlers.

Robinia pseudo-acacia [19]   Black Locust (erroneously, Honey Locust)

164

In dry upland woods, pastures, waste land, along streams statewide. Blooms in May and June.

A large tree, to 70 feet (21 m), with zigzag twigs.

Flowers, in long racemes, are white with a yellow splotch on the standard and have the typical pea-flower shape. They are very fragrant and can be eaten.

Leaves are compound with from 9 to 19 oval leaflets, rounded at tip and base, drooping and folding in the evening.

The small, stout spines are found only on the fast growing twigs. The true Honey Locust with large thorns in bunches is *Gleditsia triacanthos*, also a member of the Pea Family.

Fruit is a pod with 4 to 8 kidney-shaped seeds.

The tree sends out underground root suckers which emerge as shoots far from the parent tree. The roots have a licorice-like flavor.

The Black Locust is often badly damaged and killed by borers. The wood is the strongest of any North American tree and is highly rot resistant.

Robinia, in honor of two French botanists named Robin; *pseudo-acacia,* "false acacia."

Schrankia uncinata [71]   Sensitive Brier

In rocky glades, open woods, along roads statewide except northwest and southeast. Blooms from May to September.

A trailing or creeping plant of dry places, all branches covered with hooked barbs.

Flowers are in ball-shaped heads composed of many funnel-type pink to rose-purple flowers with long stamens protruding. Long flower stalks arise from leaf axils.

Leaves are double compound with 13 to 15 leaflets which are again divided into 8 to 16 very small leaflets called pinnules. The pinnules are less than 1″ (25 mm) long and very slender. The small leaflets can fold up and close.

Fruit is a very prickly pod to 3½" (9 cm) long.

Schrankia, for Franz von Schrank, a German botanist of the 19th century; *uncinata*, Latin for "hooked" or "barbed," referring to the prickles on stems and leaves.

Stylosanthes biflora [42]   Pencil Flower

In open woods and glades in acid soils, mainly south of the Missouri River. Blooms from May to September.

A low plant with wiry branches up to 20" (45 cm) long, which trail or ascend, emerging from the base or above.

Flowers are few, mainly terminal, clear yellow to orange or, rarely, cream, about ⅜" (1 cm) long, carried in pairs or single. The "flag," the broad upper petal, is rounded. The calyx-tube has an unusual stalk-like shape and the flower stalk is subtended by partially united stipules, forming a tube around the stem.

Leaves are compound-trifoliate, the leaflets on very short stems. Leaflets either pointed or rounded, narrow or oblong to 1½" (4 cm) long.

Stylosanthes, Greek, "pillar flower," referring to the calyx tube; *biflora*, Latin, "two-flowered," though single flowers are quite common. "Pencil Flower" refers to the same characteristic as the generic name.

165

Tephrosia virginiana [65]   Goat's Rue, Hoary Pea, Wild Sweet Pea, Devil's Shoe String, Cat-gut

Rocky open woods, glades, prairies, in acid soils south of the Missouri River, scattered in the north part of the state. Blooms from May to August.

A showy member of the Pea Family, 12" to 24" (30 to 60 cm) high.

The flowers in spikes, each flower about ¾" (18 mm) long, have yellow standards suffused with pink while the keel is rose-pink.

Leaves are pinnately divided into 14 to 28 narrowly oblong, opposite leaflets similar to Mimosa or Sensitive Plant.

The entire plant is so downy that it appears grey.

Seeds are in small, pea-shaped pods.

The roots contain rotenone, a deadly poison for cold-blooded animals, and were used by Indians to poison fish.

Tephrosia, from Greek *tephros*, "ash-colored" or "hoary."

Vicia villosa [82]   Hairy Vetch, Winter Vetch

In fields, waste places, along roads and railroads, scattered statewide. Blooms from April to October. Native of Europe.

Spreading, to 2½ feet (75 cm) high, forming a dense ground cover.

Flowers are in long-stemmed clusters all along the stem, arising from leaf
axils. From 8 to 20 flowers, pointing to one side of the stalk, each flower
½″ to ¾″ (12 to 18 mm) long, typically pea-flower shaped. Colors range
from rich lavender to purple or violet to whitish.

Leaves are divided into many narrow leaflets with tendrils at the end of
the leaf.

Stems are very hairy, as are inflorescences.

Fruit is a pod about 1″ (25 mm) long.

It was introduced agriculturally from Europe and has naturalized all over
the U.S.

166 *Vicia* is the classical Latin name for Vetch; *villosa*, Latin for "hairy."

Vicia caroliniana Wood Vetch

In rocky areas on acid soils in the Ozarks. Blooms from April to June.

A trailing or climbing smooth plant, similar to *V. villosa* but flowers are
white to off-white and the keel is tipped with blue or lilac.

WOOD SORREL FAMILY *Oxalidaceae*

Oxalis violacea [64] Violet Wood Sorrel

In rocky open woods, prairies, glades, along roads, usually in acid soils,
statewide. Blooms from April to July, sometimes again in the fall.

Flower stalks with many 5-petalled flowers grow to 8″ (20 cm) high.
Flowers are light magenta or lavender, sometimes white—but never
violet.

Leaves, on stems lower than the flowers, are 3-divided into heart-shaped
leaflets. Leaves can close up along the central vein of the leaflets.

The root is a small, scale-covered bulb from which the flower and leaf
stalks arise.

Oxalis, Greek for "sharp," from the sour taste caused by oxalic acid;
violacea, Latin for "violet."

Oxalis stricta [36] Yellow Wood Sorrel, Sheep Sorrel, Lady's Sorrel

In rocky open woods, fields, waste ground, along roads and railroads statewide. Blooms from May to October.

Plants are 6″ to 8″ (15 to 20 cm) tall, greyish-green and downy. Flowers
and leaves arise from common axils.

Yellow flowers have 5 rounded petals and each flower is about ⅝″ (16
mm) across. They appear in unequally branched umbels on long
stems.

Leaves, 3-divided like field clover with heart-shaped leaflets, also grow on
long stems along the plant stalk. They are light to dark green or in
shades of copper to purple.
Oxalis contains oxalic acid which gives it a sour taste.
Oxalis, Greek for "sharp;" *stricta*, Latin for "erect."

GERANIUM FAMILY *Geraniaceae*

Geranium maculatum [62]   Wild Geranium, Crane's Bill, Spotted Crane's Bill

In rich or rocky open woods, borders of woods, statewide except southeast
lowlands. Blooms from April to June.
Plants about 2 feet (60 cm) tall, frequently found growing in colonies
and near the borders of woods.
Flowers are 5-petalled, 1" (25 mm) across, in colors from deep magenta-
pink to very light purple with petals pencilled with darker streaks.
The 10 pollen-bearing anthers often wither and fall off before the
stigma is ready for fertilization, so insects, mostly bees, are necessary
for seed production.
Prominently toothed, opposite leaves, deeply cut into 5 lobes, have brown
and white spots. Upper leaves are 3-lobed or whole.
The fruit forms a sharply pointed "crane's bill," one of the common names
for the Geraniums.
Geranium, Greek for "crane" or "heron;" *maculatum*, Latin for "spotted."

167

Geranium carolinianum   Carolina Cranesbill

In waste places, fields, statewide. Blooms from May to July.
Small flowers, light pink, about ½" (12 mm) across with 5 petals.
Leaves deeply cleft into 5 lobes which are themselves much lobed.

RUE FAMILY *Rutaceae*

Ptelea trifoliata [13]   Hop Tree, Wafer Ash

On limestone glades, prairies, open woods, valleys in south, central, and
northeast Missouri. Blooms from April to June.
A small tree.
Flowers are very small, in clusters, greenish-white, with 4 petals and 4
sepals.
Leaves are alternate, compound, 3-divided, spear shaped, pointed at both
ends. The family to which *Ptelea* belongs is part of the citrus tribe
and *P. trifoliata's* leaves have an orange-like fragrance.

The fruit is 2 seeds in a round, paper-like envelope which is veined. The unripe seeds have been substituted for hops in beer making.

The bitter, aromatic roots have been used as a substitute for quinine.

The flowers and bark give off a skunk-like odor when bruised.

Ptelea, Greek for "elm," refers to the elm-like fruit; *trifoliata,* Latin for "three-leaved."

SPURGE FAMILY *Euphorbiaceae*

168

Euphorbia corollata [23] Flowering Spurge

On prairies, glades, open woods, along roads and railroads statewide. Blooms from May to October.

This is a tall plant, to 3 feet (90 cm) high, with a much branched top. On glades and in poor soil it has only a few flowers on small plants. But in rich soil very large plants—as wide as high—arise, each covered with hundreds of flowers.

The 5-lobed white inflorescence, only a little over ¼″ (6 mm) across, is botanically a "petal-like appendage." The reproductive structure of Euphorbia is entirely different from plants of other families.

Leaves are oblong, without stems, alternate, forming a whorl wherever the stem branches. On terminal branches the leaves are opposite.

All *Euphorbia* species exude a milky, acrid juice when bruised and are poisonous to animals when eaten.

Euphorbia, Greek, believed to have been named for a physician to King Juba; *corollata,* Latin, "with a corolla."

Euphorbia commutata [52] Wood Spurge

In woods, valleys, along streams in central and eastern counties. Blooms from April to June.

A common early spring plant of the Ozarks, to 12″ (30 cm) or somewhat taller.

Inflorescences are greenish-yellow, in compact clusters on stems which emerge from a whorl of symmetrical, rather large, rounded floral leaves. In addition, each flower is subtended by two small, green bracts which are also round.

Leaves along stems are alternate, sessile, short and rounded.

All green parts contain a white, milky juice which may irritate the skin.

Euphorbia, Greek, for the physician of King Juba; *commutata,* Latin, "changing."

OTHER EUPHORBIA SPECIES

Twenty species of *Euphorbia* are found in Missouri; 12 have a limited distribution.
In addition to the two species pictured, there are 6 others which are commonly found.

Euphorbia obtusata   Blunt-leaved Spurge

In low woods, fields, valleys, scattered in south, central, and east-central counties. Blooms from late May to July.
Plants to 18″ (45 cm) tall on straight stems.
Inflorescences are light green.
Leaves are without stems, alternate, narrow oblong. The leaf-like bracts below the inflorescences are opposite.

169

Euphorbia heterophylla   Painted Leaf or Wild Poinsettia

In valleys, fields, waste places, roadsides statewide except the southeast and some northern counties. Blooms from July to October.
To 3 feet (90 cm) tall, but usually lower.
Inflorescences insignificant, green.
Leaf shapes, even those on one plant, extremely variable; wide and lobed or linear, with or without teeth. Upper leaves below inflorescense often red or with red base.

Euphorbia marginata   Snow-on-the-Mountain

Though native, usually escaped from cultivation, scattered. Blooms from June to October.
To 3 feet (90 cm) tall with very hairy stems.
Stem leaves broadly ovate to 1¼″ (3 cm) wide. The uppermost leaves and those at the base of the inflorescences with wide white margins.

Euphorbia dentata   Toothed Spurge

In prairies, fields, waste places, roadsides statewide. Blooms from July to October.
To 15″ (38 cm) tall, often branched.
Inflorescences interspersed with small leaves.
Leaves dull green, hairy, somewhat triangular with coarse teeth, opposite on long stems.

Euphorbia maculata   Nodding Spurge

In fields, waste places, roadsides statewide. Blooms from May to October.
Hairy plant which spreads, often with dark red stems, on the ground.

Inflorescences inconspicuous.

Leaves are opposite, often blotched, about ⅝″ (16 mm) long.

Euphorbia supina   Milk Purslane

In fields, waste places, roadsides statewide. Blooms from May to October.

A common ground-hugging weed of dry places.

Stems, often red, radiate in all directions from a central root in a circular spread.

Leaves very small, dull green with a central red spot and fine teeth at the margins.

170   CASHEW FAMILY *Anacardiaceae*

Rhus glabra [54]   Smooth Sumac

In upland prairies, old fields, along roads and railroads statewide. Blooms from late May to July.

A smooth, hairless shrub, rarely a small tree, that forms thickets by root suckers.

Flowers are in dense, pyramidal, upright clusters to 7″ (18 cm) long, greenish-yellow in color.

Leaves are alternate, compound, with 9 to 27 leaflets. Leaflets are opposite and terminal, spear-shaped, pointed with fairly large teeth. In August the leaves turn bright red on the upper surface and are silvery-white below.

The fruit is in clusters of small berries, bright rose-red at first, turning to maroon brown later. A tea can be brewed from the astringent berries which are also eaten by animals and birds, including turkeys.

Indians made flutes from the stalks, a dye from the berries, used the twigs and leaves, which are rich in tannin, for treating leather, and smoked the leaves.

Rhus, an old Greek and Latin name; *glabra,* Latin for "smooth" or "without hair."

Rhus copallina   Winged or Dwarf Sumac

Usually on acid soils, borders of woods, fields, glades, statewide except northern counties. Blooms from May to November.

Differs from *R. glabra* in that the branches and leaf stalks are covered by a fine hairiness, leaves are not toothed, and the leaf-axis is winged in the space between the leaflets.

Rhus aromatica   Fragrant Sumac

In open woods, glades, borders of woods statewide. Blooms in March and

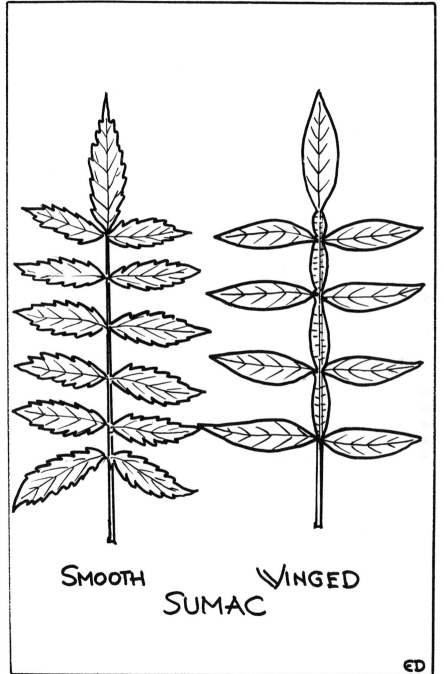

SMOOTH   WINGED
SUMAC

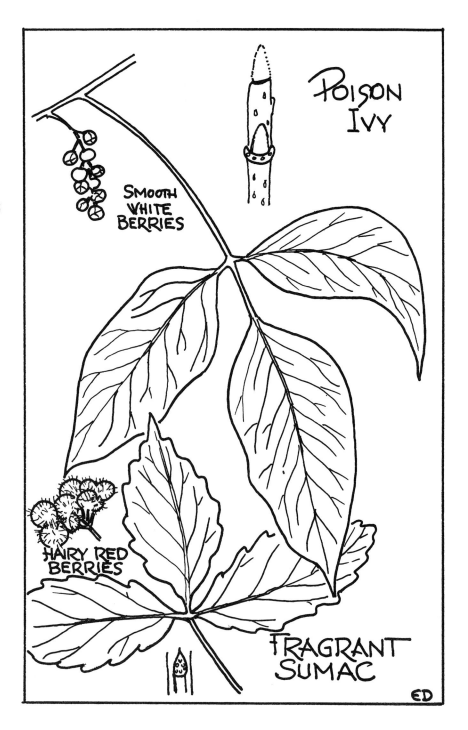

POISON IVY

SMOOTH WHITE BERRIES

HAIRY RED BERRIES

FRAGRANT SUMAC

ED

April.

A low shrub, to 3 feet (90 cm) tall.

Small yellow flowers in clusters, often before leaves appear.

Leaves 3-divided, rounded.

Middle leaflet is without a stem, while the middle leaflet of Poison Ivy, *R. radicans*, is on a long stem.

Fruit, which appears from May to July, is a bright red, hairy "drupe" much esteemed by birds.

All parts of the plant are pleasantly aromatic. It is a good garden subject.

Rhus radicans [54]   Poison Ivy

In fence rows, open woods, waste ground, along roads and railroads state-wide. Blooms from May to July.

Either a vine with aerial roots or a shrub to 10 feet (3 m) high.

Flowers are in spikes arising from leaf axils, white or greenish-white, very small, with 5 petals and 5 sepals.

Leaves are 3-divided—"Leaves three, let it be"—the two laterals on very short stems and the middle leaflet on a much longer stalk. Leaflets are large, wavy, ovate with rounded bottom, pointed to sharply pointed, with or without a few large teeth.

The fruits are white, sticky berries which are eaten by many birds.

The poison is a volatile oil which gets on the skin through contact with the plant or smoke from a fire. Wash as soon as possible after suspected contact, preferably with hot water or alcohol.

The terms Poison Ivy and Poison Oak are used for the same plant, though Poison Oak properly applies to *Rhus toxidodendron*, a low-growing shrub, never a climber, found only in the southern-most counties of Missouri.

Rhus, an old Greek and Latin name; *radicans*, Latin for "climbing."

BLADDER-NUT FAMILY *Staphyleaceae*

Staphylea trifolia [9]   American Bladder-nut

In rich woods, along streams, usually in limestone, statewide except southeast lowlands. Blooms in April and May.

A shrub, rarely a very small tree.

Flowers hang bell-like in small clusters. The flower shape is somewhat like Lily of the Valley, with the stamens sticking out of the bell.

Leaves are dark green, 3-divided, the leaflets egg-shaped with elongated points, finely toothed. Leaves are opposite.

The fruit is an inflated bladder-like envelope, somewhat like a bishop's tiara but with the 3 points at the bottom, which encloses 1 to 4 light brown seeds which rattle in the bladder.

Staphylea, from Greek *staphyle* or "cluster;" *trifolia*, Latin, "three-leaved."

MAPLE FAMILY *Aceraceae*

Acer rubrum [61]   Red Maple

In bottomlands, but sometimes on rocky hillsides and bluffs of south and southeast Missouri. Blooms in March and April.

A tree with an oval top, rarely over 60 feet (18 m) tall where it has space to spread, but often much taller when growing in forests.

The striking flowers unfold before the leaves. Male flowers are red, female are orange. Male and female flowers may appear either on the same tree or on separate trees.

The leaves are 3-lobed, sometimes with two additional small lobes near the base.

Fruit, winterbuds, twigs, and unfolding leaves are all red.

The Maples are important "understory" trees of our upland Oak-Hickory forests, but are primarily a bottomland tree.

Acer, the classical Latin name for Maple; *rubrum*, Latin for "red."

HORSE CHESTNUT FAMILY *Hippocastanaceae*

Aesculus glabra [35]   Ohio Buckeye

On limestone hillsides with moist soil statewide except southeast lowlands. Blooms in April and May.

A common understory tree, though specimens up to 75 feet (23 m) tall occur.

Flowers are large, upright clusters, yellow to greenish-yellow, at the end of branches.

Leaves are compound with star-shaped clusters of leaflets, 5 in number, 3″ to 6″ long (7.5 to 15 cm), broad ovate, and pointed at both ends. Side veins are parallel. A rare subspecies with from 7 to 11 leaflets exists.

It is one of the first trees to leaf out in spring. Leaf buds are spectacularly large and beautiful.

Bark of old trees is furrowed and scaly, grey in color.

The fruit is a nut, about 1″ (25 mm) in diameter, which is poisonous when eaten.

Aesculus, Latin name for some mast-bearing trees; *glabra*, Latin for "smooth" or "without hair."

174

TOUCH-ME-NOT FAMILY *Balsaminaceae*

Impatiens capensis [41]   Spotted Touch-me-not, Jewelweed

In damp, low woods, near streams, swampy areas statewide. Blooms from
late May to October.

Plants to 5 feet (1.5 m) high on weak, watery stems which are much
branched.

Orange-colored flowers, each hanging from a slender stem, resemble
cornucopias with the end of the horn turned under.

Leaves are soft, deep bluish-green, alternate, egg-shaped, coarsely toothed,
to 3½″ (9 cm) long.

The fruit is a slender capsule which, in drying, contracts and splits ex-   **175**
plosively, casting seeds far away in all directions.

Touch-me-not can take over large areas of wet ground.

Impatiens, Latin for "impatient," referring to the explosive fruit; *capensis*
refers to the Cape of Good Hope, but the reason isn't known.

It is widely believed that rubbing leaves and stems of *Impatiens* on the
skin will prevent and even cure Poison Ivy infection. Recent scientific
research indicates some basis for this belief.

Impatiens pallida   Pale Touch-me-not

All information is the same as for *I. capensis* but flowers are pale yellow
and leaves narrower.

BUCKTHORN FAMILY *Rhamnaceae*

Ceanothus americanus [16]   New Jersey Tea

In open woods, upland prairies, glades statewide. Blooms in May, occasionally again in the fall.

A low shrub to 3 feet (90 cm) tall.

Upright clusters of tiny white flowers, the clusters somewhat like small
Lilac blossoms, grow at the end of the branches or arise out of the
leaf axils.

Leaves are hairy, especially on the under side, alternate, oval, toothed, and
pointed.

During the American Revolution a tea was brewed from the leaves which,
however, do not contain caffein. Deer browse the shrubs.

Ceanothus, an obscure ancient Greek name.

Ceanothus ovatus   Redroot or Inland New Jersey Tea

On prairies and uplands in western counties only. Blooms from late April
to June.

Similar to *C. americanus,* but a lower shrub with dense, flat-domed flower clusters and narrower leaves.

GRAPE FAMILY *Vitaceae*

Vitis vulpina [54]   Winter Grape, Frost Grape, Chicken Grape

Low, wet woods, along streams statewide except southeast lowlands. Blooms in mid-May and June.

A rampant climber with stout, woody stems.

The tiny, pleasantly scented, light green flowers are clustered on branching infloresences.

176 The leaves are large, 6″ to 8″ (15 to 20 cm) long and almost as wide, heart-shaped, with coarse teeth.

The grapes become sweet only after frost. They are eaten by birds and wild animals.

Vitis, the classical Latin name for Grape; *vulpina,* Latin for "little fox," as Br'er Fox loves grapes.

There are 8 species of Grapes in Missouri, of which 5 are widely distributed. **V.** *vulpina* was chosen to represent these important climbing plants. All other Grapes differ mainly in leaf shape.

MALLOW FAMILY *Malvaceae*

Sida spinosa [48]   Prickly Sida, Prickly Mallow

In fields, waste places, along roads and railroads statewide. Blooms from June to October. Native of Eurasia and Africa.

A small, much branched plant to 18″ (45 cm) high.

Flowers grow along the stem in the axils of the leaf stems. They are dull orange-yellow, ⅓″ (8 mm) across, typical Mallow flowers with 5 petals and joined stamens and pistil, as in the Hollyhock.

Leaves are on very long stems, heart-shaped, to 3″ (75 mm) long, with fairly coarse teeth.

Sida, from an old Greek name given by Linnaeus; *spinosa,* Latin, "spiny," for the small projection at the base of the leaf stalk which looks like, but is not, a spine.

Hibiscus lasiocarpos [75]   Rose Mallow

On borders of lakes, sloughs, ponds, in ditches in southern and southeast Missouri. Blooms from July to October.

Tall, perennial herbs, sometimes with woody stalks, usually 6 to 8 feet high (1.8 to 2.4 m).

The flowers of *H. lasiocarpos* and *H. militaris* are nearly identical. The 5 large petals form a disc-shaped inflorescence with a 6″ (15 cm) spread, the largest wild flower in Missouri. Colors are white or rose with a central large spot of wine-purple.

Leaves are large, somewhat heart-shaped, either lobed or not.

Seeds are eaten by ducks and quail.

Hibiscus forms extensive colonies. To see more than a thousand flowers at one time is a splendid sight.

Hibiscus, Greek and Latin name for some kind of Mallow; *lasiocarpos*, Greek, "rough-fruited," for the large, tough seed capsules.   **177**

Hibiscus militaris   Halbert-leaf or Rose Mallow

In ditches, lakes, swamps, absent from the Ozarks and northeast counties. Blooms from July to October.

Similar to *H. lasiocarpos*, but leaves are lance (halbert) shaped.

ST. JOHN'S-WORT FAMILY *Hypericaceae*

Ascyrum hypericoides [49]   St. Andrew's Cross

In dry, open woods on acid soils south of the Missouri River. Blooms from July to October.

A very low shrub which has its northernmost distribution in Missouri, with much branched, flattened, slightly woody stems and branches, to 10″ (25 cm) high.

Flowers are bright lemon yellow with 4 petals in the position of the St. Andrew's cross, an oblique cross. The 4 sepals are unusual as 2 are quite large and the other 2 minute. Typical of the *Hypericum* genus, there are many stamens.

Leaves opposite, sessile, lighter green below, narrowly oblong to 1″ (25 mm) long.

Ascyrum, Greek, "not rough," probably the ancient name of some plant, possibly of this Family; *hypericoides*, Greek, "like a *hypericum*," another genus of the Family.

Hypericum perforatum [42]   Common St. John's-wort

In fields, waste ground, along roads and railroads, scattered statewide. Blooms from early May to September.

Shrub-like, to 3 feet (90 cm) tall, much branched with leafy shoots.

Flowers in clusters, deep yellow, to 1″ (25 mm) across with many stamens on long ligaments, a characteristic of the St. John's-wort Family. Petals have tiny black spots.

Leaves are opposite, 1″ to 3″ (25 to 75 mm) long, narrow oblong, without stems.

Hypericum, a Greek name of obscure meaning; *perforatum*, Latin for "pierced," referring to the many translucent spots on the leaves.

Hypericum spathulatum [45]   Shrubby St. John's-wort

In either dry or moist places, gravel bars, wooded slopes, absent from the northwest one-third of the state. Blooms from June to September.

A densely branched shrub to nearly 8 feet (2.4 m) high, wide-spreading with woody, two-edged twigs.

Flowers many, mostly terminally in flat-topped clusters, bright yellow with 5 petals, to ¾″ (18 mm) across. A mass of spreading stamens makes the flower very attractive.

Leaves opposite, sessile, lustrous, somewhat leathery, oblong lanceolate to 3″ (75 mm), but usually shorter.

Hypericum, a Greek name of obscure meaning; *spathulatum*, Latin, "spatula-like," points to the shape of the leaves.

Hypericum punctatum   Dotted St. John's-wort

On waste ground, fallow fields, roadsides, statewide. Blooms from June to September.

To 3 feet (90 cm) tall from a woody base.

Flowers small, crowded, the petals with conspicuous black dots.

Leaves ovate to lanceolate, either partially clasping the stem or with short petioles or no petioles.

Hypericum sphaerocarpum   Round-podded St. John's-wort

Dry or moist places statewide. Blooms from May to September.

Simple or branching plant to 2½ feet (75 cm) tall.

Flowers terminal, either yellow or orange.

Leaves opposite, narrow and blunt, to 3″ (75 mm) long.

Hypericum mutilum   Dwarf St. John's-wort

In wet, open places scattered statewide, absent from northern counties. Blooms from July to October.

A low, much-branched plant to about 12″ (30 cm) tall.

Flowers are small, about ³⁄₁₆″ (5 mm) wide, either yellow or orange.

Leaves sessile, clasping, obtuse, about 1″ (25 mm) long.

Hypericum drummondii   Nits-and-lice

In fields, prairies, rock outcroppings, generally south of the Missouri River.

Blooms from June to September.
Bushy-branched, about 12″ (30 cm) high, sometimes taller.
Flowers very small, scattered along upper parts of branches.
Leaves linear, opposite to 1″ (25 mm) long.

Hypericum gentianoides   Pine-weed

On acid soils and rock outcroppings, scattered in the Ozarks. Blooms from
   July to October.
Shrub-like, low, not over 1 foot (30 cm), much like *H. drummondii* but
   leaves reduced in size to scale-like appearance.

179

VIOLET FAMILY *Violaceae*

**All violets bloom in early spring, some as early as March, some as late
as June. But April and May are the months of their prime.**

Hybanthus concolor [52]   Green Violet

On wooded slopes and bluffs, usually on limestone, mainly south of the
   Missouri River. Blooms from April to June.
A leafy plant of from one to many stalks, normally to 2 feet (60 cm) tall,
   but sometimes taller.
Flowers small, light green, hang on short stems which curve down from
   leaf axils; sepals are linear and very short. Five petals are of equal
   length but the lowest petal is twice as broad as the others and swollen
   at the base (gibbous). The characteristic spur of other Violets is
   missing.
Leaves are many, alternate, oblong lanceolate, pointed at the tip and also
   toward the base, to 4½″ (11.5 cm) long.
Fruit is a capsule, resembling a tiny watermelon, composed of three valves
   which split open to expose the surprisingly large seeds.
Hybanthus, Greek, means "hump-backed flower," referring to the swollen
   base of one of the petals; *concolor*, Latin, "of one color," as both leaves
   and flowers are green.

Viola pedata [83]   Bird's-foot Violet, Pansy Violet, Hens and Roosters

In rocky, dry, open woods, glades, along roads, nearly always in acid soil,
   in eastern, southern, and central Missouri, scattered in the north.
   Blooms from April to June, sometimes again in fall.
Grows to about 3½″ (9 cm) high.
Flowers are to 1″ (25 mm) across, in two major color patterns: 1) the

upper 2 petals deep purple velvet, the 3 lower ones pale lilac or lavender; or 2) all 5 petals uniformly pale lilac or lavender. A third form, clear white, is very rare. Even rarer is a pattern of deep purple upper petals with the lower 3 petals snow white. The center is always orange.

Leaves are deeply dissected like a "bird's foot." Later, during early summer, a new set of leaves develops which are still dissected, but the ribbons are much wider.

To see thousands of these handsome "Pansy Violets" along roads is one of the most rewarding sights of spring. *V. pedata* takes over areas which have been disturbed, but cannot stand competition and slowly disappears as other plants intrude.

180

Viola, classical Latin name for Violet; *pedata,* Latin, "foot-like," for the leaves.

Viola sororia [79]   Woolly Blue Violet, Downy Blue Violet

In open woods, borders of woods, along streams statewide. Blooms from March to June.

This is a very common Violet, one of seven "blue" Violets in Missouri.

Leaves are heart-shaped and scalloped. Stems and underside of leaves are conspicuously hairy.

Viola, classical Latin name for Violet; *sororia,* Latin for "sisterly," because it looks so much like other Violets.

Other "Blue" Violets

A) With entire leaves:

Viola papilionacea Meadow Violet

In rich, moist places statewide.

Very similar to *V. sororia* but leaves and stems are smooth, without hair.

Viola missouriensis Missouri Violet

In rich, moist places statewide.

Flowers usually above leaves. Corolla pale violet with a darker band above the white center.

Leaves triangular with rounded bottom lobes.

Viola sagittata Arrow-leaved Violet

In open but variable situations, in a broad band diagonally across Missouri from southwest to northeast.

Flowers as high as leaves. Leaves arrow-shaped, the basal lobes with 2 or 3 large teeth.

VIOLA

PAPILIONACEA

PEDATA

MISSOURIENSIS

SORORIA

VIOLA

SAGITTATA

VIARUM

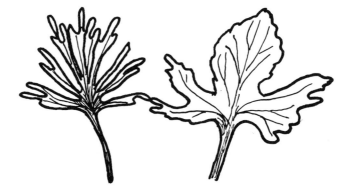

PETATIFIDA   TRILOBA

B) With incised leaves:
Viola viarum   Plains Violet
In moist, usually low places, throughout Missouri except the southeast lowlands.
Flowers are lower than leaves.
Leaves either entire with round-toothed edges or deeply 3 to 7-lobed, or parted with an asymetrical outline.

Viola triloba   Three-lobed Violet
On acid soils in dry, upland woods, but also near streams, south of the Missouri River and in northeast counties.
Flowers lower than leaves.
Early leaves often round and scalloped. Later leaves irregularly 3-lobed and coarsely toothed. A 5-lobed form is fairly common.

183

Viola pedatifida   Prairie Violet
On prairies of western and northern Missouri.
Flowers are showy, deep purple.
Leaves are deeply incised with very narrow segments.

Viola rafinesquii [79]   Johnny-jump-up

In fields, meadows, glades, along roads and railroads, absent from northern-most counties. Blooms from March to May.
Much branched, 3″ to 4″ (75 mm to 10 cm) high.
Flowers are typical Violet-shaped, a washed out blue, light yellow or white in the center.
Leaves are ½″ to ¾″ (12 to 18 mm) long, rounded and irregularly scalloped. Each leaf has a large stipule which looks like the spread tail of a bird.
This very low growing Violet, a very early flowering announcer of spring's arrival, carpets entire fields.
Viola, classical Latin name for Violet; *rafinesquii*, for Samuel Constantine Rafinesque Schmaltz who lived from 1783 to 1840.
The name of this Violet is given by several authors as V. *kitaibeliana*, honoring professor Paul Kitaibel, a botanist and chemist at the University of Budapest in Hungary (1757-1817).

Viola pensylvanica [30]   Smooth Yellow Violet

In rich low woods, slopes, river bottoms statewide. Blooms from March to May.
The only yellow violet in Missouri, each flower grows on a separate terminal stalk. The 3 lower petals have purple veins.
Both basal and stem leaves are heart-shaped and finely scalloped.

Viola striata   Pale or Striped Violet

In moist woods and bottomlands, absent from northern and western counties. Blooms from April to June.

Flowers are white or cream with very narrow stripes of blue on lowest petal.

Leaves are entire, heart-shaped, finely toothed.

Becomes quite rank, to 18″ (45 cm) as the season progresses.

Two other White Violets occur in Missouri, *V. pallens* and *V. lanceolata*, both very rare.

184

CACTUS FAMILY *Cactaceae*

Opuntia compressa [38]   Prickly Pear

On glades, rocky prairies, along streams and railroads in south and central Missouri. Blooms from late May to July.

This is the only Cactus species growing wild in Missouri. What appear to be leaves, the rounded or oblong fleshy segments, are actually thickened stems which hug the ground. The real leaves are soft little protuberances near the upper part of the stems, about ¼″ (6 mm) long, surrounded by spines and small, hairlike bristles which are most irritating to human skin. The leaves persist only a short time.

Flowers are numerous, bright yellow, often with a large orange spot at base of petals, to 3″ (75 mm) across, with 8 to 12 petals and many stamens. As most Cacti live in the desert and must attract the attention of the few extant insects for fertilization, they often present gorgeous, brilliantly colored flowers.

The edible fruits are dull purplish-red, pear-shaped, with tufts of bristles. The seeds are imbedded in a mucilaginous substance.

Opuntia is a name used by Pliny nearly 1,500 years before America was discovered. Since all Cacti are of American origin, he must have been talking about some other plant. The Latin word *compressa* means "compressed," referring to the stem sections.

LOOSESTRIFE FAMILY *Lythraceae*

Lythrum alatum [72]   Winged Loosestrife

In wet prairies, swamps, glades, in ditches and margins of ponds and sloughs statewide. Blooms from early June to September.

A perennial, 2 to 3 feet (60 to 90 cm) tall, with very leafy stems.

The flowers are small, about ¼″ (6 mm) across, deep magenta in color with 5 to 7 petals. They arise from the leaf axils.

Leaves are without stalks, the lower ones opposite or in whorls of three. The upper leaves, rounded at the base and tapering to a point, become progressively smaller toward the plant top.

The stem is four-sided.

Lythrum, Greek, means "clotted blood," referring to a European species of that color; *alatum,* Latin for "winged," referring to the branches which have marginal angles. Loosestrife is a mistranslation of the Greek word *Lysimachia.*

EVENING PRIMROSE FAMILY *Onagraceae*

Ludwigia alternifolia [45]   False Loosestrife, Seedbox   **185**

In wet places, borders of swamps, sloughs, in ditches, wet meadows and prairies statewide. Blooms from June to August.

A branching plant about 18″ (45 cm) tall.

Single, lemon yellow flowers with 4 rounded petals are carried in leaf axils. The 4 green calix lobes, as large as the petals, remain after the petals have fallen.

Leaves are lance-shaped, to 4″ (10 cm) long, sharply pointed, tapering at the base into short stems.

This is a relative of the Evening Primroses and the flowers look very similar.

Ludwigia, named for a German botanist of the 18th century, C. G. Ludwig; *alternifolia,* Latin for "alternate leaved."

Gaura biennis [25]   Gaura, Butterfly Flower

On prairies, glades, fields, roadsides statewide. Blooms from June to October.

A tall plant, to 5 feet (1.5 m) high, much branched toward the top.

The flowers, carried on spikes at the end of the branches, have 4 petals which are white at first but turn pink with age. These petals are about ½″ to ¾″ (12 to 18 mm) long and all point upward. In contrast, the 8 stamens curve downward, giving the flower the appearance of a small butterfly in flight.

Leaves are stalkless, to 4″ (10 cm) long, lance-shaped, with widely spaced teeth.

Gaura, Greek, means "stately;" *biennis,* Latin, indicates the plant completes its life cycle in 2 years.

Oenothera biennis [45]   Evening Primrose

In fields, prairies, waste land, along roads and railroads statewide. Blooms from June to October.

This is a robust, much branched plant, to 6 feet (1.8 m) tall with leafy stems. It is a common sight in weed patches and along roads.

As the common name indicates, flowers open very suddenly in late afternoon and close early the next morning. They are fertilized by night-flying moths, but also by bees and bumble bees. The flowers are pale yellow, with 4 rounded petals, about 2″ (5 cm) across. The stigma of all Evening Primroses is prominently 4-lobed.

Leaves are alternate, light green, without stems, elliptical to lance-shaped, with or without teeth, to 6″ (15 cm) long.

Oenothera, Greek for "wine scented," the fragrance of the flowers; *biennis,* Latin, means the plant completes its life cycle in 2 years.

186

Oenothera speciosa [68]   Showy Evening Primrose

In prairies, fields, waste ground, along roads and railroads in southern and central counties, rare in the north. Blooms from May to July.

A low growing plant, 6″ to 12″ (15 to 30 cm) high.

Flowers are large, to 3″ (75 mm) across, with white or pink petals.

Leaves are small, broad-toothed and wavy, lance-shaped, to 3″ (75 mm) long.

Originally a western prairie dweller, *O. speciosa* is now widely distributed, often covering the right-of-way of roads with a pink carpet.

Oenothera, Greek for "wine-scented," referring to the perfume of the flowers; *speciosa,* Latin for "showy."

Oenothera missouriensis [37]   Missouri Evening Primrose

In limestone glades and bluffs of the Ozark region north to the Missouri River. Blooms from May to August.

A low growing, sprawling plant of the glades.

The large, lemon-yellow flowers, to 3½″ (90 mm) across, have 4 overlapping petals. They open in late afternoon and close when the sun hits them in the morning. On cloudy days they often stay open until noon or even later. As the flower fades it turns to shades of pink-orange. The flowers arise from leaf axils.

Leaves are alternate, lance-shaped, many on one stem.

The fruit is showy with 4 broad wings.

Oenothera, Greek for "wine-scented," referring to the perfume of the flowers.

Oenothera laciniata   Cutleafed Evening Primrose

In fields, waste places, roadsides, absent from northern counties. Blooms

from May to October.
Normally a low-growing plant, but sometimes to 2 feet (60 cm) tall.
Small, pale yellow flowers.
Leaves deeply incised, dandelion-like to 2″ (50 mm) long.

Oenothera linifolia   Sundrops or Thread-leafed Sundrop

In fields, prairies, roadsides, generally south of the Missouri River. Blooms
from May to July.
Either single-stemmed or branched, to 18″ (45 cm) high.
Small, yellow flowers in spike-like arrangement.
Leaves are thread-like to linear.

187

PARSLEY FAMILY *Apiaceae* (*Umbelliferae*)

Daucus carota [21]   Queen Anne's Lace, Wild Carrot, Bird's Nest Plant

In fields, waste ground, roadsides, statewide. Blooms from May to October. Native of Eurasia.
To 5 feet (1.5 m) tall, much branched, with a stout taproot.
Flowers minute, 5-petalled, white or rarely pinkish, in large compound
umbels. The central floret of the inflorescence usually purple.
Leaves pinnately divided into strap-like leaflets (decompound). The rosette of basal leaves is formed during the first year and over winter;
the flower stalk develops during the second growing season.
As the inflorescence withers the umbel contracts to form a bowl into
which the seeds fall, thus the name "Bird's Nest." Seeds are oblong
and spiny.
This troublesome weed, difficult to control, is one of the ancestors of the
cultivated carrot.
Daucus is the Greek and *carota* the Latin name for carrot.

Erigenia bulbosa [1]   Harbinger of Spring, Pepper and Salt

In rich woods near the base of slopes, along streams in valleys of the Ozark
region, southern and east-central counties. Blooms from January to
April.
At first only a few inches high, the plant will ultimately reach to 8″ (20
cm).
A few warm days in mid-winter and *Erigenia* opens the flowering season.
Little white flowers, each with 5 petals, in small umbrella-shaped
clusters (umbels) push up through last year's fallen leaves. Red-brown
anthers show prominently, giving the name Pepper and Salt.

Leaves are divided fern-like and usually come out some time after flowering begins.

The root is a small, ball-shaped tuber.

The plant is very tender and it is hard to understand how it escapes freezing to death.

Erigenia, Greek *ery-geneia*, "early-born," a charming name given by Homer to Eos, the goddess of the dawn.

Eryngium yuccifolium [55]   Rattlesnake Master, Yucca-leaf Eryngo, Button Snakeroot

On glades, prairies, rocky open woods statewide except southeast lowlands. Blooms in July and August.

Tall, stiff, upright-growing stems to 4 feet (1.2 m) tall, with global flower heads.

The flowers are greenish-white.

The bluish, basal leaves have bristles along their margins and grow to 3 feet (90 cm) long. Leaves emerging along the stems are much smaller and clasping.

It is difficult to imagine that this large plant with the leaves of a Yucca is closely related to the Wild Carrot or the tiny Harbinger of Spring.

Eryngium, Greek, is the name given by Theophrastus to some type of Thistle; *yuccifolium*, "with the leaves of a Yucca." The common name Rattlesnake Master is also used for *Agave virginica*.

Osmorhiza claytoni [10]   Sweet Cicely, Wooly Sweet Cicely

On rich wooded slopes and bottomlands statewide except southeast low lands. Blooms from April to June.

An herb to 3 feet (90 cm) tall.

Minute white flowers are massed in umbels.

Leaves are 3-divided and the leaflets are divided again—fern-like.

The entire plant is downy.

The root is shaped like a small carrot. The root and leaves are aromatic, smelling like anise or licorice.

Osmorhiza, Greek for "aromatic root;" *claytoni*, probably for John Clayton, an 18th century botanist from Virginia.

Osmorhiza longistylis   Anise Root

All data the same as for *O. claytoni*, except that leaflets are not as deeply cleft.

Pastinaca sativa [37]   Parsnip

In fields, waste places, along roads and railroads of west, north, and central

Missouri. Blooms from May to October. Native of Europe.
Grows to 4 feet (1.2 m) tall with fleshy stems.
The yellow flowers are very small in compound umbels.
Leaves are pinnately divided. That is, opposite leaves are spaced along a common stem. Leaflets are 3 to 5-lobed, toothed.
This is probably the same plant as the cultivated Parsnip which is grown for its edible roots.
Pastinaca, Latin *pastus* means "food;" *sativa,* Latin for "cultivated."

Thaspium trifoliatum [39]   Meadow Parsnip

On prairies, rocky open woods, ledges and bluffs, common south and scattered north of the Missouri River. Blooms from April to June.
A much branched plant to 2½ feet (75 cm) high.
Flowers are in a compound umbel in a flat inflorescence. They are dark yellow, very rarely purple or brownish purple. The central flower in each little umbel is raised, a distinguishing characteristic from a very similar plant, *Zizia* or Golden Alexander.
Basal leaves are either undivided or divided into egg-shaped or lance-shaped, long-stalked leaflets 1" to 2" (25 to 50 mm) long. Leaves along the stems are 3-divided, egg-shaped, with rounded base. All leaves are finely toothed.
Thaspium is a word play on *Thapsium,* another genus of the Parsley Family; *trifoliatum,* Latin for "3-leaved."

189

Thaspium barbinode   Hairy-jointed Meadow Parsnip

All data the same as for *T. trifoliatum* except that flowers are creamy or pale yellow, and the 3-divided leaves have large teeth.

Torilis japonica [14]   Hedge Parsley

On waste ground, roadsides, railroads, fields statewide. Blooms from June to August. Native of Eurasia.
Much-branched plants to 2½ feet (75 cm) tall with inflorescences well raised above the leaves.
Flowers on long stems (peduncles) in compound umbels, the umbels on short stems to 1" (25 mm) long. Individual flowers minute with 5 petals and 5 stamens.
Leaves doubly pinnate (feather-like), parsley-like.
Fruit is densely covered with hooked prickles which cling firmly to clothing and fur.
Torilis, a name of unknown origin.
The plant arrived in Missouri after 1900 but now covers large areas, es-

pecially where Man has disturbed the land, giving Hedge Parsley a chance to get started.

DOGWOOD FAMILY *Cornaceae*

Cornus florida [9]   Flowering Dogwood

On wooded slopes, ravines, bluffs, on well drained soil, generally south of the Missouri River and in counties adjoining it. Blooms from mid-April to mid-May.

190 The state tree of Missouri and possibly the favorite spring-flowering tree, it is commonly an understory tree in oak-hickory hardwood forests. It is usually a small tree, but specimens with a diameter to 8″ (20 cm) are known.

The true flowers are the insignificant looking yellowish clusters which are surrounded by the 4 large, notched, petal-like bracts of pure white tipped with brown-purple. Pink flowered Dogwoods are very rare in the wild.

Leaves are egg-shaped, to 5″ (13 cm) long, pointed at both ends. They show a rare form of veining (arcuate), with the secondary veins running parallel to the edges of the leaves.

Fruits are borne in clusters of brilliant scarlet, berry-like drupes, each holding two seeds. Birds love the fruits, especially robins, mockingbirds, and wild turkeys.

The bark is reddish-tan to brown, broken into an overall pattern of scales. The wood is very strong and shock resistant.

Do not attempt to transplant Dogwood from the wild. Their roots are far reaching and are severly damaged in digging, weakening the tree which easily falls victim to the attack of borers.

Cornus, Latin for "horn," because of the wood's hardness.

Cornus obliqua [20]   Swamp Dogwood, Pale Dogwood, Silky Dogwood

In lowlands, along streams, wet prairies statewide except southeast lowlands. Blooms from May to July.

A large shrub. The easiest clue to identification of this species is the association with wet situations.

Typically flat or slightly curved clusters of many small flowers.

Leaves are opposite, somewhat narrower than those of other Dogwoods.

The fruit, blue, berry-like drupes, may be present from June through October. The fruit of this and all other Dogwoods is eaten by many birds.

Cornus, Latin for "horn," from the hardness of the wood; *obliqua,* Latin for "oblique" or "awry," referring to the asymetrical shape of the stone-fruit.

Cornus drummondii   Rough-leaved Dogwood

Usually in dry, but sometimes moist places statewide. Blooms in May and June.
Flowers are small, white, in flat or domed clusters, similar to *C. obliqua.*
Leaves are opposite, hairy on both sides, rough above, the underside "wooly."
Fruit is a white, berry-like drupe.
This plant tolerates very dry conditions.

191

Cornus racemosa   Gray Dogwood

In moist lowlands, scattered statewide. Blooms from May to July.
Flowers are small, white, in domed clusters. Inflorescence domed nearly as high as wide.
Leaves are opposite, very similar to but more ovate than *C. obliqua.*
Fruit is white on red stems.
Branches are grey, as indicated by the common name.

Cornus alternifolia   Alternate-leaf Dogwood

On north facing slopes and stream banks, scattered in the eastern half of the state. Blooms from May to July.
Flowers are small, white, in flat or domed clusters.
This is the only Dogwood with alternate leaves. Leaves are crowded at the ends of branches, appearing whorled. They are pale and whitened on the underside.
Fruit is blue-black on reddish stalks.

HEATH FAMILY *Ericaceae*

Rhododendron roseum [63]   Azalea, Rhododendron, Honey-suckle

On north facing slopes and along streams in acid soils of the southeast and southern Ozarks. Blooms from late April to late May.
A woody shrub to 7 feet (2.1 m) high.
The flowers are large, about 3" (75 mm) across, and bunched terminally on the branches. Individual flowers have 5 wavy, petal-like lobes with long stamens and even longer pistil protruding. Colors are pink, rose, deep rose, and quite rarely, white. They are very fragrant.

Leaves are to 6″ (15 cm) long, leathery, smooth, broadly ovate, in groups.
While the natural habitat is in shaded ravines and valleys, *R. roseum* will
　do equally well in full sun if soil and drainage conditions are proper.
Natives use the name Honeysuckle exclusively.
Rhododendron, Greek for "rose tree;" *roseum*, Latin for "rose-colored."

Vaccinium stamineum [13]   Deerberry, Highbush Huckleberry, Squaw Huckleberry

In dry, rocky, open woods, upland slopes and glades, in acid soils of the
　Ozark region. Blooms from April to June.

192

A shrub to 10 feet (3 m) tall.
Flowers are single or in small clusters, each flower stalk with a small leaf
　(bract).
The flowers are white, bell-shaped, with 5 pointed lobes surrounded by
　a green calyx and the joined stamens and pistil protruding noticeably.
　They hang downward. The many flowers make the shrub lovely in
　bloom.
Leaves are alternate, ovate, on stems, to about 3″ (75 mm) long.
The berries are edible, though not very tasty raw. They are desirable for
　marmalade or jellies.
Vaccinium, classical Latin name for Blueberry; *stamineum*, Latin, "with
　prominent stamens."

Vaccinium arboreum   Farkleberry or Tree Huckleberry

Habitat, distribution, and appearance very similar to *V. stamineum*, but
　it blooms much later, from July to October.
Stamens and pistils do not protrude from the bell-shaped, white flowers.

Vaccinium vacillans [13]   Lowbush Blueberry

In dry, rocky, open woods, upland flats, in acid soils of the Ozark region
　and east-central counties. Blooms in April and May.
A low shrub with many stiff branches, usually not over 12″ (30 cm) high,
　but sometimes much higher.
Flowers, in small clusters along the stems, hang downward like little
　bells which are longer, about ⅜″ (10 mm), than they are broad. They
　show a whitish color with a green calix.
Fruit is a bluish-black berry, sweet-sour, edible. They ripen a few at a
　time and are never plentiful. Animals enjoy them.
Vaccinium, the classical Latin name for one of the Blueberries; *vacillans*,
　Latin, "swaying," referring to the little bell flowers.

PRIMROSE FAMILY *Primulaceae*

Anagallis arvensis [71]   Pimpernel, Poor Man's Weatherglass

In fields, pastures, waste places, along railroads in central and east-central Missouri. Blooms from May to September. Native of Europe.

A dwarf, delicate plant with stems not much over 6″ (15 cm).

Flowers single on long stems, scarlet or brick-red, rarely white, botanically tubes with 5 lobes, but the tube is so short as to be hardly noticeable. Flowers open only in sunshine and close around 4 o'clock and also whenever clouds approach. Thus, "Poor Man's Weatherglass," a name originally from England.

Leaves stemless, opposite, and rarely in threes, ovate with dots underneath.

193

Fruit is a rounded capsule which opens a "lid" to disperse its seeds.

Anagallis, Greek, two words, "again" and "to delight," pointing to the re-opening of the flowers when the clouds have passed; *arvensis,* Latin, "of the meadows."

Dodecatheon meadia [62]   Shooting Star

On prairies, glades, ledges and bluffs, rocky wooded slopes in eastern, central, and southern Missouri. Blooms from April to June.

Leafless flower stalks, to 2½ feet (75 cm) tall, arise from a basal rosette of smooth, lance-shaped leaves to 10″ (25 cm) long.

The Shooting Star is well named. The flowers are reminiscent of a meteor with its spreading tail. Five long pink or white petals turn outward and upward while the stamens protrude in a beak-like cone from the center of the flower. The flowers grow in clusters or umbels.

Dodecatheon, Greek for "twelve gods;" *meadia* is in honor of Dr. Richard Mead, 1673-1754.

Lysimachia lanceolata [39]   Loosestrife

In dry or wet rocky woods, wet areas on prairies, absent from northwest counties. Blooms from May to August.

The plant is about 18″ (45 cm) tall.

Flowers of this and other Lysimachias have a pleasing shape. The 5 yellow petals are broad and pointed, about ¾″ (16 mm) across. The flowers are carried on long, slender stems at the end of the stalk and arise out of a whorl of leaves.

Leaves are lance-shaped, tapering at both ends, but lower leaves are ovate. They are opposite and form whorls, with small leaves emerging from the axils of the larger leaves.

Lysimachia is believed to be named after Lysimachos, king of Thrace. Loosestrife is a mistranslation of the Greek *Lysimachia.*

Lysimachia ciliata   Fringed Loosestrife

In moist woods and meadows statewide. Blooms from May to July.
Rarely to 4 feet (1.2 m) high.
Flowers very similar to *L. lanceolata,* but petals slightly fringed and the leaf-stalks (petioles) have long, eyebrow-like hair.
Leaves to 6″ (15 cm) long, ovate, very finely toothed.

194

GENTIAN FAMILY *Gentianaceae*

Gentiana andrewsii [91]   Closed Gentian

In low woods, along streams, below bluffs, in ravines, scattered south of the Missouri River. Blooms from August to October.
Stems to 18″ (45 cm) tall.
Flowers are bottle or club-shaped, to 2″ (50 mm) long, which never open. They grow in tight clusters out of leaf axils. Varying colors, from violet-blue to deep wine red, are often found on the same plant.
Leaves are ovate lance-shaped, dark green with a prominent center vein.
We associate the Gentian Family with alpine or sub-alpine scenery, but Missouri has five Gentian species, all with a fairly wide distribution, though none are common.
Gentiana, for King Gentius who is supposed to have discovered medicinal properties in some Gentians; *andrewsii,* for English botanist Henry C. Andrews, 1794-1830.

Sabatia angularis [72]   Rose Gentian, Rose Pink

On glades, upland fields, open woods, usually in acid soils in southern, northeastern and east-central counties. Blooms from late June to September.
Rarely grows over 2 feet (60 cm) high, with many opposite branches, somewhat like a candelabra, and with angled and squared stems.
Flowers to 1″ (25 mm) across, terminal on many stalks, with 5 petal-like corolla lobes. The color is pink or, less frequently, white.
Leaves are opposite, heart-shaped, clasping at the base, to 1½″ (40 mm) long.
Sabatia, for Liberato Sabbati, 18th century Italian botanist; *angularis,* Latin for "angular," referring to the stems.

Sabatia campestris   Prairie Rose Gentian

On prairies, fallow fields, along roads, scattered in the southern two-thirds
of Missouri. Blooms from July to September.

Grows lower than *S. angularis*, to 9″ (23 cm) tall, and in different habitat.

Calyx-lobes are as long or longer than the corolla segments. Flowers are
pink.

Leaves are sessile, opposite, ovate lanceolate; those of *S. angularis* are
nearly triangular.

Swertia caroliniensis [53] *(Frasera)*   American Columbo

In rich low woods, wooded valleys, along streams of southeast Missouri.
Blooms in May and June.

195

A very leafy plant to 8 feet (2.4 m) tall forming spectacular colonies.

The inflorescence is pyramidal, frequently 24″ (60 cm) long, with greenish-white flowers, about 1″ (25 mm) across, which are dotted with
brown-purple and have a large gland on each of the 4 petals.

Leaves are in whorls on the stalk, oblong-narrow. Basal leaves are very
large, to 18″ (45 cm) long, lance-shaped.

Individual plants do not bloom for years, showing only the basal rosette of
leaves. The plant dies after flowering.

Swertia, for Emanual Swert, a 17th century Dutch horticulturist.

DOGBANE FAMILY *Apocynaceae*

Amsonia illustris [85]   Blue Star

On gravel bars, moist areas near bluffs and creeks in southern and eastern
Missouri. Blooms in April and May.

A striking plant, forming clumps 18″ to 3 feet (45 to 90 cm) high on
gravel bars.

Flowers are light blue, in panicles at the top of stems.

Leaves are oblong, lance-shaped, shiny on the upper surface.

Amsonia, for Charles Amson, an 18th century physician from Virginia;
illustris, Latin for "bright."

Another species, *A. tabernaemontana*, grows in rich, moist, open woods
and has leaves which are dull on the upper surface.

Swallowtail Butterflies love the *Amsonias*, particularly the Zebra Swallowtail shown in the picture.

Apocynum cannabinum [23]   Indian Hemp, Dogbane

On prairies, glades, waste areas, open woods statewide. Blooms from May
to August.

Upright perennial plants, to 3 feet (90 cm) tall, with opposite leaves and branches.

Flowers are off-white in clusters at the end of branching stems. Individual flowers are small with a 5-lobed corolla. They are very attractive to bees.

Leaves are smooth-edged, oblong or lance-shaped, without stalks.

All parts of the plant exude an acrid, white juice when bruised. The Family is closely related to Milkweeds.

The stem has tough fiber bark which has been used, like hemp, for making rope. The plants have medicinal use.

Apocynum, Greek meaning "away dog" or "dog poison;" *cannabinum*, Latin, "like hemp."

196

Apocynum medium   Intermediate Dogbane

In borders of woods, prairies, scattered statewide. Blooms from May to July.

Flowers are white or tinged with pink. Floral lobes are spreading, not recurved.

Leaves are broader than *A. cannabinum* with a more spreading base.

Apocynum androsaemifolium   Spreading Dogbane

All data the same as for *A. medium,* but shrub-like and the pink flowers are nodding with recurved lobes.

MILKWEED FAMILY *Asclepiadaceae*

The genus *Asclepias* of the Milkweed Family is represented by 15 species in Missouri, of which 9 have wide distribution.

The Milkweeds, so called for the poisonous milky juice in the green parts of most species, give us some of the showiest plants and flowers through the summer.

They attract large numbers of butterflies, especially the Swallowtails and Fritillaries, but are fertilized by bees and bee-like insects and are host plants to the larvae of certain butterflies which depend on them for food.

The flowers are unique in shape and give the impression of two flowers joined back to back. See pages 108-109, for a detailed floral description.

The flowers have a waxy appearance and are borne in spreading, often rounded, crowns.

The silky floss of the seeds—miniature parachutes—is a familiar sight floating in the fall breezes. The "silk" has been used as a substitute for kapok.

Asclepias quadrifolia [65] Four-leaved Milkweed

In rich or dry, open woods, usually upland, absent from the northwest one-third of the state. Blooms from May to July.

Normally about 12″ (30 cm) high, but sometimes taller, this woodland Milkweed is more graceful than other members of the genus and blooms earlier.

Flowers in one to three umbels carried terminally. They have the typical erect crown, known as the "hood," and reflected corolla lobes. They vary from deep pink to white and are delicately fragrant.

197

Leaves are on long stems (petioles). One set, near the middle of the stem, is often a whorl of four, giving the plant its species name. But this feature is frequently missing. Other leaves in sets of two, opposite. All leaves are lanceolate, tapering to a point at the tip and toward the petiole.

Asclepias, the Greek god of healing; *quadrifolia,* Latin, "four-leaved."

Asclepias tuberosa [40] Butterfly-weed

In fields and dry glades, waste places, statewide. Blooms from late May to September.

The showiest of all Milkweeds, to 3 feet (90 cm) tall with flat-topped masses of brilliant orange flowers on a much branched inflorescence. The very rare yellow form should be protected rigorously.

Leaves are hairy, narrow, lance-shaped, dark green, on very short stems.

The conspicuously long seed pods burst in late fall showing the spirally, tightly packed seeds which are later released and wind-borne on their silky floss.

The plant likes dry, hot places and is often found in ground which has previously been disturbed.

Asclepias, Greek god of healing; *tuberosa,* Latin, "swelling," referring to the roots.

Asclepias purpurascens [67] Purple Milkweed

In rocky, open woods, meadows, along roads and ditches statewide except southeast lowlands. Blooms from May to July.

Grows to 3½ feet (1.1 m) tall.

The crimson or crimson-magenta, but never purple, flowers are borne in umbels on stout, usually single, stalks.

The heavy, pointed, opposite leaves are on very short stalks. They have a fine downy covering on the under side.

Asclepias, Greek god of healing; *purpurascens*, Latin, "becoming purple."

Asclepias syriaca [67]   Common Milkweed

In fields, waste ground, along roads and railroads statewide. Blooms from May to August.

A very stout, coarse plant to 4½ feet (1.4 m) tall, it is the most common of our Milkweeds.

Flowers are dull crimson-pink to brownish-lilac, very fragrant, borne in clusters on top and along stems, arising from leaf axils.

Broad, oblong leaves are thick, opposite, on short stems. Leaves are yellowish-green, leaf ribs are yellow.

Large seedpods with soft protuberances contain tightly packed seeds provided with silky down parachutes.

Asclepias, Greek god of healing; *syriaca*, the plant was erroneously thought to have been introduced from the Middle East.

Asclepias viridis   Green-flowered Milkweed

On glades and rocky prairies, primarily south of the Missouri River. Blooms in May and June.

Plants to 2 feet (60 cm) high.

Flowers with lower half (corolla lobe) green, upper half (crown) purplish.

Leaves on short stems, oblong, to 5″ (13 cm) long.

Asclepias viridiflora   Green Milkweed

On glades and rocky prairies statewide except some northern counties. Blooms from May to August.

Plants to 3 feet (90 cm) tall.

Flowers appearing to be closed, light green, in clusters both terminal and from leaf axils.

Leaves on short petioles, lanceolate, thick, to 5″ (13 cm) long.

Asclepias incarnata   Swamp Milkweed

In moist bottomland, along streams statewide except in southeast lowlands. Blooms from June to August.

Long, smooth stems to 5 feet (1.5 m) tall, branched above.

Many slightly rounded flower clusters with pink, rarely white, flowers.

Leaves narrow, lanceolate, to 6″ (15 cm) long.

Asclepias verticillata   Whorled Milkweed

In dry prairies, fields, roadsides, statewide. Blooms from May to September.

Flower clusters of greenish-white flowers are terminal on unbranched stems to 2½ feet (76 cm) tall.

Leaves linear, thread-like, in whorls.

Asclepias hirtella   Florida Milkweed

On prairies and glades, absent from the Ozarks and southeast lowlands. Blooms from May to August.

To 3 feet (90 cm) tall.

Another Milkweed with greenish-white flowers in dense clusters arising from the leaf axils. Flowers much smaller than *A. viridis* or *A. viridiflora*.

Leaves almost linear-lanceolate, rough. The lower surface of the leaves shows conspicuous side-nerves and veins.

199

Cynanchum laeve [27]   Angle-pod

On cultivated land, gardens, roadsides, thickets, statewide except south-central counties. Blooms from July to September.

A perennial, vigorous climber which covers fences and shrubs.

Flowers small, in many clusters (cymes) which arise on long stems from the leaf axils. Flower envelope (calyx) 5-divided, corolla lobes twice as long as calyx, deeply cleft and pointed. They have a strong scent.

Leaves to 7" (18 cm) long, dark green, heart-shaped, on long stems.

Fruit a silky floss- and seed-filled pod, typical of the Milkweed Family. These pods often stay on the dead vines through winter to open on a warm day in early spring.

Cynanchum, Greek, the name of some plant which was used to kill, actually "strangle," dogs; *laeve,* Latin, "smooth."

The plant has been recommended as food for bees, but would become an uncontrollable nuisance in a short time.

Matelea decipiens [58] *(Gonolobus)*   Climbing Milkweed, Angle-pod

In rocky open woods, glades, along streams, in the Ozark region north to the Missouri River. Blooms in late May and June.

A climbing or trailing vine.

Flowers are a deep chocolate brown, in clusters arising from leaf axils.

Leaves are large, heart-shaped, usually near 5" to 6" (13 to 15 cm) long.

Matelea is the native name of a vine growing on Martinique which, for some unknown reason, was given to this Climbing Milkweed; *decipiens,* Latin for "deceiving," possibly because the flower structure differs so much from the characteristic floral shape of the Milkweed Family.

MORNING GLORY FAMILY *Convolvulaceae*

Convolvulus sepium [17]   Hedge Bindweed

In valleys, along roads and railroads, waste places, scattered statewide but absent from the southeast. Blooms from May to September.

200   A native creeping and climbing plant, spreading by deep roots, hugging the ground. An intruder which is very difficult to eradicate.

Flowers are one to a stem, to 2″ (5 cm) long, open white chalices or light pink with white stripes. Each flower has at its base two leaf-like bracts, an easy identification feature.

Leaves are arrow-shaped with rather blunt basal lobes, to 5″ (13 cm) long.

Convolvulus, Latin, "to entwine;" *sepium,* Latin, "of hedges or fences."

Convolvulus arvensis   Field or Small Bindweed

Habitat, distribution, and flowering time are the same as *C. sepium,* as are the flowers. Native of Eurasia.

But this species has no bracts beneath the flowers.

Leaves smaller than *C. sepium* and basal lobes are more pointed.

Ipomoea pandurata [18]   Wild Potato Vine, Man-of-the-Earth

In fields, along streams, roads and railroads statewide. Blooms from May to September.

Long, trailing stems to 15 feet (4.5 m), but also climbing to 10 feet (3 m) high.

Flowers are funnel-shaped, to 3″ (75 mm) long, white, but sometimes shades of purple or rose, with a dark crimson or purple center.

Leaves are heart-shaped, from 2″ to 6″ (5 to 15 cm) long.

The tuber-like, fleshy root may grow to 2 feet (60 cm) in length and as thick as a person's leg, weighing 20 pounds or more. It often branches, giving the appearance of legs. Indians boiled and ate the roots.

Through the Middle Ages there was a tendency to see in parts of plants a resemblance to human shapes and to ascribe magic powers to such fancied andromorphous plants.

Ipomoea, a word invented by Linnaeus from two Greek words to mean "like a bindweed;" *pandurata,* Latin for "fiddle-shaped," referring to the leaves which sometimes vary from the heart shape.

PHLOX FAMILY *Polemoniaceae*

Phlox bifida [80] Sand Phlox

In rocky, dry upland woods, along streams, on slopes in acid or lime soils in the southeast Ozarks and north-central counties. Blooms from March to May.

To about 6″ (15 cm) high, spreading and forming creeping mats.

Flowers pale or rose-purple, very rarely all white, about ½″ (12 mm) across, each petal with a deep notch, the lobes forming a rounded V shape.

Leaves many, linear, opposite, very light green.

The geographic distribution of this plant is unusual.

Phlox, Greek, "flame;" *bifida*, Latin for "twice cut," the corolla lobes.

201

Phlox divaricata [80] Blue Phlox, Wild Sweet William

In rich and rocky woods, often in wet areas along streams, statewide except southeast lowlands. Blooms from April to June.

To 12″ (30 cm) high, normally in partial shade.

Flowers are tubes with 5 petal-like lobes which are either pointed or notched, about ¾″ (18 mm) across. Colors are lilac, rose-lavender, purple, blue, or very rarely white.

Leaves are opposite, lance-shaped, spaced along the stems. Dark green leafy shoots spread from the base and take root.

Phlox, Greek, "flame;" *divaricata*, Latin for "spreading."

Phlox pilosa Downy Phlox

Appearance, habitat, distribution, and flowering time like *P. divaricata*, though in east-central counties *P. pilosa* blooms somewhat later than *P. divaricata*.

Note the spreading hair on stems and leaves, while *P. divaricata* is smooth.

Flowers can be rose, red-purple, violet, white, or white with a purple center.

Phlox paniculata [76] Perennial Phlox

At the borders of rich woods, along streams, below bluffs, in the Ozark region and in northeast counties. Blooms from July to October.

This late summer and fall flowering Phlox grows from 2 to 4 feet (.6 to 1.2 m) tall.

Flowers in dense pyramidal and terminal clusters are rose-purple, deep pink, or white. Many selections have been made for horticultural use.

Leaves are oblong or lance-shaped, conspicuously veined, opposite.

Phlox, Greek for "flame;" *paniculata*, Latin, "in panicles," referring to the arrangement of the flowers.

Polemonium reptans [81]   Jacob's Ladder, Greek Valerian

In upland or low woods, near streams in rich soil, statewide except northwest counties. Blooms from April to June.

Low, weak-stemmed plants to about 15″ (38 cm) long.

Flowers are light blue or blue-lavender, 5-lobed tubes, bell-shaped, in loose terminal clusters.

Leaves are alternate, pinnately compound, with ovate, opposite, smooth leaflets.

202

Jacob's Ladder is from the ladder-like arrangement of the leaflets.

Polemonium, Greek proper name; *reptans*, Latin for "creeping."

WATERLEAF FAMILY *Hydrophyllaceae*

Hydrophyllum appendiculatum [61]   Woolen Breeches

In rich woods, on steep slopes, in wooded valleys, statewide except southwest counties. Blooms from April to July.

A bristly and hairy plant to 2 feet (60 cm) tall.

Flowers, grouped above the foliage, are delicate, light blue bells from which the purple-tipped stamens protrude only slightly.

Thin leaves, soft hairy, palmately 5-lobed with coarse teeth, on long petioles.

Hydrophyllum, Greek, "water leaf," as the leaves of this genus are often blotched as if spotted by water; *appendiculatum*, Latin, "appendaged," because the bristly-hairy sepals of this species have tiny reflected appendages between them.

Hydrophyllum virginianum   Waterleaf

Habitat, distribution, and flowering time the same as *H. appendiculatum*.

The main difference is in the leaves which have from 3 to 7 divisions of which the lowest division is separated from the others by a section of leaf-stem.

Hydrophyllum canadense   Broadleaf or Canada Waterleaf

Habitat is the same as *H. appendiculatum*. Distributed only in eastern counties, mainly along the Mississippi River. Flowers from May to July.

A smooth plant, not hairy.

CANADENSE

LONG PETIOLE

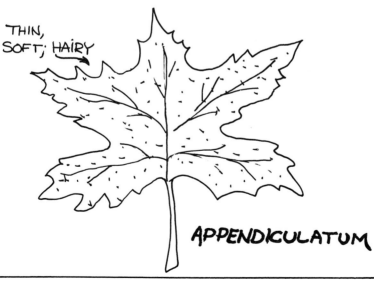

THIN, SOFT, HAIRY

APPENDICULATUM

HYDROPHYLLUM VIRGINIANUM

Flowers usually borne below leaves. Stamens long, protruding from the corolla.
Leaves palmate with coarse teeth, some on very long petioles.

Phacelia purshii [84]   Phacelia, Miami Mist, Pursh's Phacelia

In low rich woods bordering streams, in moist places of east-central and southeast Missouri. Blooms from April to June.
Delicate, finely hairy plants, 12″ to 18″ (30 to 45 cm) high, much branched with slender stems.
From 8 to 30 flowers, each about ½″ (12 mm) across, grow in terminal clusters. The flowers have 5 lobes which are minutely fringed. The color is very light violet or whitish, with a large white "eye" with tiny dots in the center.
Leaves 1½″ to 3″ (40 to 80 mm) long, are deeply lobed into segments which are opposite along a central vein.
Phacelia, Greek, "cluster," referring to the flowers; *purshii*, for Frederick Traugott Pursh, 1774-1820, who discovered the plant.

205

Phacelia gilioides   Small-flowered Phacelia

In variable habitat on open ground south of the Missouri River. Blooms from April to June.
Similar to *P. purshii* but flowers are not fringed.

Phacelia hirsuta   Hairy Phacelia

Habitat and flowering time the same as *P. gilioides.* Distribution is limited to southwest counties.
Usually stouter and larger than preceding species, and with hairy stems and leaves.

BORAGE FAMILY *Boraginaceae*

Cynoglossum virginianum [84]   Wild Comfrey, Giant Forget-me-not

On rich or rocky wooded slopes or bottomlands of central and southeast Missouri. Blooms from April to June.
Flower stalk to 2½ feet (76 cm) tall with a few clasping leaves, arising from a basal rosette of leaves.
Flowers look like small Forget-me-nots, with small tubes ending in 5 rounded lobes, about ½″ (12 mm) across. Their color is a pale, washed-out blue or violet or greenish-white.
Basal leaves are very conspicuous, to 12″ (30 cm) long, oval-lanceolate,

tapering into long stems. All green parts of the plant are softly hairy. Fruits are 4 round nutlets, depressed on the upper surface, prickly-hairy. They attach themselves to man and beast.

Cynoglossum, from *cyno,* Greek for "dog," and *glossum,* Latin for "tongue." "Hound's tongue" is a good description of the soft, flappy leaves.

Echium vulgare [87] Viper's Bugloss, Blue-weed

On gravel bars, in ditches, along roads and waste ground, scattered in north, central, and eastern Missouri. Blooms from May to September. Native of Europe.

Many stems from a common root, carrying flowers, leaves, and stiff bristly hair, to 2½ feet (76 cm) tall.

Flowers along the upper part of the stalks, on one side of spikes, unfurl from a tight coil. This arrangement is typical of the Borage Family. The individual flowers are funnel-shaped tubes with uneven lobes, to ¾″ (20 mm) long, ranging from pink buds to light blue and ultramarine-violet, with protruding pink stamens. A white form exists but has not yet been reported from Missouri.

Leaves are very slender, stemless, bristly on both sides. The dense hairyness gives the plant a silvery appearance.

Echium, Greek for "viper," a fancied resemblance of the fruit-nutlets to a snake's head; *vulgare,* Latin for "common." Bugloss is an English word given to a number of European herbs of the Borage Family.

Lithospermum canescens [29] Puccoon, Hoary Puccoon, Orange Puccoon

In dry open woods, glades, prairies, along roads and railroads statewide except in southeast lowlands. Blooms from March to June.

Many stalks 6″ to 12″ (15 to 30 cm) tall, hairy, from one root system.

Flowers are orange to orange-yellow, rarely pale yellow, borne in clusters at the end of the stem. Flower spikes are curved with flowers beginning to bloom from the lower end, a characteristic of the Borage Family. Flowers are tubes with 5 lobes.

Leaves are slender, alternate, pointing upward, and very hairy.

Lithospermum, Greek for "stone-seeded;" *canescens,* Latin, means "grey-hairy." Puccoon is an Indian word.

Lithospermum incisum Yellow Puccoon

On prairies, roadsides, glades, scattered in central and western Missouri. Blooms from April to June.

Similar to *L. canescens,* but flowers are yellow, not orange, and not as closely grouped. The lobes are delicately fringed.

Lithospermum arvense   Corn Gromwell

In fields, waste places, roadsides, missing from northern and southernmost counties. Blooms from April to June.

Rough, hairy, to 18″ (45 cm) high.

Flowers are minute, white, almost hidden by bracts, with 5 petals. The flowers are reminiscent of Forget-me-not which belongs to the same Family.

Leaves are alternate, lance-shaped, without petioles.

Mertensia virginica [80]   Bluebells, Virginia Cowslip, Lung-wort

In rich woods on slopes or in river bottoms, scattered statewide except in the northwest and southwest. Blooms from March to early June.

Plants to 2 feet (60 cm) tall.

Flowers in loose clusters at the top of the stems, with flaring tubes, about 1″ (25 mm) long, hanging bell-like. Pink buds turn light blue on opening. A pink variety is very rare in Missouri, and truly white specimens are also rare.

Leaves are large, soft, bluish-green, oval to nearly round, the larger ones to 5″ (13 cm) long.

This is the only totally hairless (glabrous) member of the Borage Family in Missouri.

Franz Carl Mertens, 1764-1831, after whom the plant was named, was a German botanist.

VERVAIN FAMILY *Verbenaceae*

Lippia lanceolata [22]   Fog Fruit

In mud and gravel margins of streams, sloughs, ditches statewide. Blooms from May to September.

Low growing plants of wet places, arising from trailing stems to 12″ (30 cm) high, and forming large colonies.

Flowers in egg-shaped clusters, very small, at the top of fairly long stems which arise from the leaf axils. Colors white or light pink.

Leaves opposite, elliptical to lance-shaped, with large teeth.

Lippia is named for August Lippi, a French traveller of the late 17th century; *lanceolata*, Latin, "lance-shaped," referring to the leaves.

Verbena canadensis [60]   Rose Verbena

In glades, fields, waste places, absent from northern counties. Blooms from March to November.

Low, bushy plants, to 20″ (50 cm) tall, with many usually hairy branches.
The only spring-blooming Verbena, it is often seen on rocks and against
rock walls.

Flowers are in terminal clusters with 5 notched petals, about ½″ (12 mm)
across. Colors and color intensity vary—magenta, lavender, lilac, or
rose-red.

Leaves are opposite or whorled, deeply 3-lobed and coarsely toothed, to
3″ (8 cm) long.

Verbena, the classical Latin name for Vervain.

Verbena hastata [89]   Blue Vervain

In wet places, along streams, in sloughs, waste ground, absent from the
Ozark region. Blooms from June to October.

To 5 feet (1.5 m) tall, 4-sided and grooved stalk, usually branching toward the top, with rough hair.

Flowers in long, narrow clusters at the end of the branches. Blossoms begin
to open at the bottom of the spikes, a few at one time. The flowers
are only ⅛″ (3 mm) across, tube-shaped with 5 lobes, ranging from
deep purple or violet to light lavender or rarely white.

Leaves dark green, lance-shaped, opposite, with fine double teeth, i.e.,
teeth on teeth, to 5″ (13 cm) long, very hairy.

Verbena, the classical Latin name for Vervain; *hastata,* Latin for "spear-
shaped," referring to the lower leaves.

Verbena simplex [20]   Narrow-leaved Verbena

On glades, prairies, waste places, railroads, statewide except the northeast
corner. Flowers from May to September.

An herb, normally with many stems, about 12″ (30 cm) tall, sometimes
higher.

Flowers in spikes, carried terminally, white to light violet. Individual flowers quite small, about ¼″ (6 mm).

Leaves very narrow, tapering to a stemless base, finely toothed, to ⅝″
(15 mm) wide but usually narrowed. The narrow leaves identify the
species.

Verbena, a name given by Pliny to some sacred herb; *simplex,* Latin,
"simple."

Verbena urticifolia   White- or Nettle-leaved Vervain

In fallow fields, roadsides, waste places, statewide. Blooms from June to
October.

Tall, branched, weedy plant to 6 feet (1.8 m) tall.

Numerous narrow flower spikes with insignificant white flowers.
Leaves on petioles, oblong-lanceolate, sharply toothed.

Verbena bracteata   Large-bracted Vervain

In waste places, roadsides, scattered statewide. Blooms from April to
October.
Sprawling, dwarf, hairy plant.
Purplish-blue flowers almost hidden by foliage.
Leaves pinnately incised.

Verbena stricta   Hoary- or Mullein-leaved Vervain

209

In waste places, roadsides, statewide. Blooms from May to September.
A densely hairy plant to 2 feet (60 cm) tall.
Flowers in spikes, purple.
Leaves ovate, pointed, coarsely toothed.

MINT FAMILY *Lamiaceae (Labiatae)*

Blephilia ciliata [70]   Ohio Horsemint

In rich woods, valley bottoms, ravines, below bluffs, absent from the western one-third of the state. Blooms from May to August.
Usually an unbranched, square-stemmed plant to 3 feet (90 cm) tall.
Flowers in clusters toward the top of the stem. Each cluster arises above
ovate, pointed bracts with hairy fringes. Each flower shows the upper
and three-lobed lower lip typical of the Mint Family. Color is pale
lavender with purple spots.
Leaves are opposite, soft, either with or without stalks, and have only an
indication of teeth.
All green parts of the plant have a pleasant mint-like perfume. The basal
leaves remain green all through winter.
Blephilia, Greek, means "eye-lashes," in reference to the hairy fringes of
the bracts; *ciliata*, Latin, stands for "hairy," like eye-lashes, pointing
to the same phenomenon.

Blephilia hirsuta   Wood Mint

In cool places, ravines, wooded slopes, scattered statewide. Blooms from
late May to September.
Similar to *B. ciliata* but stems and leaves are hairy, leaves have long stems,
and they are strongly toothed.

Cunila origanoides [76]   Dittany

In dry, open woods, prairies, along bluffs in acid soils in south, central,
and east-central counties. Blooms from July to November.

Low-growing, many-branched, shrub-like with square, wiry stems to
about 12″ (30 cm) tall.

Flowers small, in tufts arising from the leaf axils, purplish or deep lavender, rarely white. Individual blossoms with a small two-lobed upper
and a broader 3-lobed lower lip.

Leaves opposite without stems, lance-shaped, broadly rounded at the
base, and with a few fine teeth.

Plant has a delightful mint scent and has been used for brewing tea.

This plant is one which forms those interesting "frost flowers" during the
first severe freeze of the winter. Water, held in the root system, is
squeezed out through cracks in the dead stems near their base and
forms ribbon-like contorted shapes of ice, sometimes to 2″ (5 cm)
wide.

The origin of the name *Cunila* is unknown; *origanoides*, Latin, means
"looking like the herb Oregano."

210

Lamium amplexicaule [60]   Henbit

On waste ground, fields, gardens, along roads and railroads, mostly south
of the Missouri River. Blooms from February to November. Native of
Eurasia and Africa.

Branching plant to 10″ (25 cm) high with square stems.

Flowers in clusters carried terminally, each cluster above a whorl of stemless leaves. The flowers have the typical lip of the Mint Family members and are bright lavender with red spots.

Leaves have stems, with the exception of those beneath the flower heads.
Those near the ground are round, while the others are more elongated.
All are bluntly toothed.

Lamium, Greek, "throat," a reference to the shape of the flower; *amplexicaule*, Latin, means "around the stem," the appearance of the upper
stemless leaves.

Lamium purpureum [61]   Dead Nettle

On waste ground, fields, gardens, along roads and railroads, common south
of the Missouri River and scattered north of it. Blooms from April to
October. Native of Eurasia.

A much branched weed to about 10″ (25 cm) high with branches curving
up or spreading low from a common root. Stems square, a key to the
Mint Family.

Flowers in clusters on top of branches above a rosette-like arrangement of of stemmed leaves. Each flower has a "lip" which gave the family its former name, *Labiatae,* from the Latin *labia,* "lip." The color is dull rose-purple. A white form exists.

Stemmed leaves are opposite, heart-shaped, bluish-green, wrinkled with scalloped margins.

Though a Mint, *Lamium* does not have a pleasant scent.

Lamium, Greek, "throat," referring to the shape of the flower; *purpureum,* Latin, "purple."

Monarda russeliana [63]   Horsemint, Wild Bergamot

In rocky, dry, open woods, glades, usually in acid soils of the Ozark region and northeast counties. Blooms from late April to June.

Square stems grow to about 3¼ feet (1 m) tall.

Flowers are clustered on top of the stalks, usually one cluster for each plant. The flower tubes, 1″ to 1½″ (25 to 40 mm) long, open into two lips; the lower broad and recurving, the upper slender, arching upward with the stamens protruding. Colors are either whitish with purple spots or pale lavender. Below the flower clusters are large, leaf-like bracts which often have purplish color.

Leaves are large, to 3½″ (9 cm) long, hairy, soft, ovate, with fine teeth. They are opposite with short stems, each pair of leaves at right angles to the nearest set.

All green parts of the plant are pleasantly aromatic. The *Monarda* is a great attraction for butterflies.

Monarda is named for the 16th century Spanish physician and herbalist, Monardes; *russeliana* refers to Alexander Russel, a British physician of the 19th century.

Monarda fistulosa   Wild Bergamot

In fields, glades, borders of woods, roadsides, statewide. Blooms from May to August.

A much branched, tall plant to 3 feet (90 cm), very prominent in summer.

Flowers lavender, lilac or rose. Bracts at base of inflorescence pale green or tinged lilac.

Leaves ovate-lanceolate, with coarse teeth.

Physostegia virginiana [70]   False Dragonhead, Obedient Plant, Lion's Heart

On prairies, glades, moist places along streams and lakes statewide. Blooms from May to September.

Perennial with several stalks to 4 feet (1.2 m) tall.

Flowers in terminal spikes, tightly spaced in vertical rows, pink to pale lilac, funnel-shaped with a hood-like upper and a 3-divided lower lip.

Leaves opposite, narrow lanceolate, sharply toothed, to 5" (13 cm) long.

Physostegia, Greek, means "bladder" and "covering," referring to the shape of the fruit. When flowers are pushed from their normal position they remain for some time where they have been turned, therefore the name Obedient Plant.

Other *Physostegia* species in Missouri are similar to *P. virginiana* and have a much more limited distribution.

212 *Prunella vulgaris* [87]   Self-heal, Heal-all

In low woods, pastures, waste ground, along roads and railroads statewide. Blooms from May to September. Native of Europe.

To 20" (50 cm) high, sometimes branched.

Flowers in a tight head which, in addition to the flowers, has many green and purplish bracts which look like small leaves. The upper lip forms a hood which covers the stamens, the lower lip is two-lobed. Colors are bluish or lavender or violet; white is rare.

Leaves egg to lance-shaped, to 4" (8 cm) long, often purplish underneath, opposite, with wavy margins.

A similar species, with slightly broader leaves, is an immigrant from Europe.

Prunella was originally "*Brunella*," origin unknown; *vulgaris*, Latin, means "common."

Pycnanthemum tenuifolium [26]   Slender Mountain Mint

In dry, rocky, open woods, fields, prairies, along streams and roads statewide. Blooms from June to September.

A much branched Mint to 3 feet (90 cm) tall with square stems.

Flowers in tight clusters at the end of branches. Individual blossoms are very small, generally white, but sometimes light lavender in color.

Leaves and bracts below flower-heads are opposite, very slender, narrow, and pointed at both ends.

All parts of the plant have a strong mint scent or, as some people declare, a sage odor.

Pycnanthemum, Greek, means "dense blossoms;" *tenuifolium*, Latin, "slender-leaved."

Pycnanthemum pilosum   Hairy Mountain Mint

All data the same as for *P. tenuifolium* except that this species has hairy stems and the leaves are wider with hair on the under side.

Scutellaria incana [89]   Skullcap

In rocky, open woods, wooded slopes, along streams in the Ozark region and north-central counties. Blooms from June to September.

To 2½ feet (76 cm) tall, stems with closely pressed-on hair.

Flowers at or near top of stalks in several spikes. Each purplish-blue blossom is about 1" (25 mm) long with an arching upper and a broad lower lip.

Leaves are opposite, to 6" (15 cm) long, the largest leaves toward the center of the stalk, ovate with rounded base and rounded teeth—almost scalloped. Underside of leaves covered with fine white hair.

Seeds are shaped like a cap, thus the name Skullcap.

Scutellaria, Latin, "dish," the shape of the sepals from which the "lips" emerge; *incana*, Latin, "hoary," referring to the leaves.

213

Scutellaria ovata   Heart-leaved Skullcap

In open woods, glades, bluffs, absent from northern counties. Blooms from May to October.

To 3 feet (90 cm) tall.

Much like S. *incana* but leaves are heart-shaped, large, with coarse teeth.

Scutellaria lateriflora   Mad-dog Skullcap

In low, wet places statewide. Blooms from June to October.

Flowers not in terminal clusters (racemes), but in one-sided racemes arising from upper leaf axils.

Leaves ovate, sharply toothed.

Scutellaria parvula   Small Skullcap

In fields, glades, prairies statewide. Blooms from May to July.

Normally lower than 12" (30 cm).

Small flowers emerge from leaf axils.

Leaves, about 1" (25 mm) long, densely hairy, with 2 or 3 scallops.

Teucrium canadense [74]   Wood Sage, American Germander

In prairies, wet meadows, low woods along streams, along roads and railroads statewide. Blooms from mid-June to September.

Hairy, straight-growing stalks to 3 feet (90 cm) tall, usually unbranched.

Flowers in dense terminal spikes. The individual flowers are lavender and have a large lower lip, while two stamens protrude from either side of the narrow upper lip.

Leaves are opposite, each pair at right angles to the adjacent ones. The leaves are lance-shaped, sharply pointed, hairy on the under surface, and more or less toothed.

Teucrium is named for Teucer, the first king of Troy.

NIGHTSHADE FAMILY *Solanaceae*

Datura stramonium [18]   Jimson Weed, Thorn Apple

In pastures, barnyards, waste or cultivated land statewide. Blooms from
May to October. Native of tropical America.

Tall, branching, leafy, rank-smelling annual, often with purple-tinged
stems, to 5 feet (1.5 m) tall.

214   Flowers are funnel-shaped, pleated and swirled, with 5 sharply pointed
lobes, to 5" (13 cm) long. The floral tube is inserted into a green
calyx less than one-half the length of the corolla. Color white to light
violet or white with a violet throat.

Flowers open in the evening, emitting an exotic perfume, and close in the
morning.

Leaves to 4" (10 cm) long, deeply lobed with teeth, carried alternately
on petioles.

Fruit is an ovoid, spiny capsule, to 2" (50 mm) high. When mature, the
capsule splits open by 4 valves to spill many flattened seeds.

**Like many other members of the Nightshade Family, *D. stramonium* is
poisonous, causing hallucinations.**

Datura, an Arabic or Hindustani name; *stramonium,* Latin, meaning unknown. This is also the name given the dried leaves which are used
pharmaceutically as a narcotic.

Physalis longifolia [41]   Ground Cherry

In rich low woods, along streams, ponds and sloughs statewide. Blooms
from May to September.

Branched perennial with smooth stems to about 12" (30 cm) tall.

Flowers bell-shaped, sulphur yellow, about 1" (25 mm) long, emerge
singly from leaf axils.

Leaves are alternate, wedge-shaped, to 3" (75 mm) long, with smooth,
unsymmetrical margins.

Fruit, the "Ground Cherry," is a berry in a crisp, paper-like husk, 5-sided
and pointed, lantern-like.

Physalis, Greek, means "bladder" and refers to the seed husk; *longifolia,*
Latin, "long-leaved."

**Of the 9 *Physalis* found in Missouri, only two others have a fairly wide
distribution.**

Physalis virginiana   Virginia Ground Cherry

In dry open places statewide. Blooms from April to July.
Normally to 2 feet (60 cm) tall, sometimes taller.
Flowers yellow with purplish spots. Stems with down-turned hair.
Leaves narrow, pointed at both ends.
Fruit red, edible.

Physalis heterophylla   Clammy Ground Cherry

In open areas, variable habitat, uplands or low places, moist or dry, statewide except central Ozarks. Blooms from May to August.
From 1 to 3 feet (30 to 90 cm) tall. Stems with sticky and spreading hair,
thus "clammy" Ground Cherry.

215

Flowers, bell-shaped, ¾" (18 mm) across, light yellow with a purplish-
brown center.
Leaves egg-shaped, to 4" (10 cm) long, with rounded base and wavy
margins.

Solanum rostratum [40]   Buffalo Bur, Kansas Thistle

On waste ground, fields, along roads and railroads statewide. Blooms from
May to October.
A drought resistant, prickly plant not over 12" (30 cm) high.
Flowers yellow, about 1" (25 mm) across, with 5 united petals which form
a scalloped, broad star from which the united stamens protrude. The
calyx, the cup from which the petals emerge, is almost concealed by
spiny prickles.
Leaves alternate, deeply lobed, with scalloped margins.
Stems completely covered with sharp bristles.
Fruit is a globe-shaped berry, entirely covered by bristles, which gets en-
tangled in the fur of wild and domestic animals.
Solanum, Latin, means to "quiet down," the effect of the extract of Nightshade on the nervous system; *rostratum*, Latin, "with a beak," referring
to one of the 5 anthers which is elongated and beak-like.
The Solanaceae include some of our most important food plants—potato,
tomato, and peppers.

Solanum carolinense   Horse Nettle

General data the same as for S. *rostratum*.
Flowers are white to bluish.
Leaves with wide, shallow lobes between points, reminiscent of an oak
leaf, while the lobes of S. *rostratum* go almost to midrib.
Yellow prickles on stems and veins of leaves.

FIGWORT FAMILY *Scrophulariaceae*

Castilleja coccinea [62]   Indian Paint-brush

In prairies, glades, swampy areas statewide except northwest and southeast lowlands. Blooms from April to July.

A plant of both dry and quite wet situations, variable in height from 8″ to 15″ (20 to 38 cm) and sometimes even taller.

The flowers are quite inconspicuous, greenish-yellow, hidden in the axils of the brightly colored bracts which vary from orange to red, rarely pure yellow, and give the plant its brilliant color.

216

Basal leaves are formed during the first year. These are short, oblong with rounded ends, while the leaves which grow alternately along the stalk are stemless, narrow with finger-like protrusions. Both types of leaves are very hairy.

This unusual plant has the ability to penetrate the roots of other plants and extract their juices, but it is not dependent on this parasitic habit.

Castilleja is named for Domingo Castillejo, a Spanish botanist; *coccinea*, Latin, "red."

Collinsia verna [82]   Blue-eyed Mary

In moist, open woods and along streams in rich soil in central Missouri. Blooms from April to June.

An annual which covers large, shaded areas in open woods with rich soil. About 15″ (38 cm) high when blooming, growing to 2 feet (60 cm) while the seeds ripen. The foliage dies by the end of June or early July.

Many flowers on each stem emerge from leaf axils. The 2-lobed upper lip is white, the 3-lobed lower lip a rich blue or sometimes violet-blue, rarely all white.

Leaves opposite, the upper ones lance-shaped, nearly stemless, while the lower leaves are broadly egg-shaped and slightly scalloped, with long stems.

Seeds germinate in late fall and the tiny, blue-green seed-leaves survive the rigors of winter.

As a garden flower, *Collinsia* self-seeds prolifically on humus-rich soil.

Collinsia is named for Zaccheus Collins, an American botanist and philanthropist, 1764-1831, of Philadelphia; *verna*, Latin, "in spring."

Gerardia tenuifolia [78] *(Agalinis)*   Gerardia

In dry or moist open woods, prairies, wet and swampy areas, scattered statewide. Blooms from August to October.

A much branched plant to 2 feet (60 cm) tall, but usually lower.

Flowers carried on slender stalks which arise from the axils of upper

GERARDIA

FLAVA

GRANDIFLORA

GERARDIA

PEDICULARIA

leaves. Colors from light magenta to rose-purple, rarely white. The flowers are tubes with 5 lobes and are ⅝″ (16 mm) long.

Leaves are very narrow, flattened, opposite, to 1¼″ (30 mm) long.

Gerardia is named for John Gerarde, an herbalist; *tenuifolia*, Latin, "narrow-leaved."

Gerardia pedicularia [51] *(Dasystoma)* Gerardia, Fern-leaved False Foxglove

In dry, rocky open woods, glades, in acid soils in the Ozark region. Blooms in August and September.

A woodland species to 4 feet (1.2 m) tall, much branched.

The flowers are hood-shaped, 1½″ to 3″ (40 to 80 mm) long tubes with prominent lobes in light yellow color. They emerge on long, hairy stalks from upper leaf axils.

219

Opposite leaves are fern-like, appearing deeply lobed but actually pinnate, meaning with small leaflets along the center vein.

Gerardia is named for John Gerarde, an herbalist; *pedicularia*, Latin, meands either "louse" or "lousy," in reference to the use of the plant to fight lice in medieval Europe. Another explanation would translate *pedicularia* as "like a Pedicularis," the Lousewort, which has leaves very similar to those of *G. pedicularia*.

Two other *Gerardias* have the same habitat, blooming time, and flowers as *G. pedicularia*, but their leaf shapes differ greatly.

Gerardia grandiflora Western False Foxglove

Absent from northwest and southeast Missouri.

Gerardia flava Downy False Foxglove

Found only in southeastern counties.

Pedicularis canadensis [31] Wood Betony, Lousewort

In dry open woods, prairies, along creeks, often in leached and acid soils, statewide except southeast lowlands. Blooms in April and May.

Often in dense clumps in acid soils. From 6″ to 10″ (15 to 25 cm) high when flowering, but to 18″ (45 cm) later.

Flowers in dense terminal clusters on unbranched stalks, light yellow or yellowish-purple. The flowers are about ¾″ (18 mm) long with a long, curved upper and a 3-lobed lower lip. The stamens follow the curve of the upper lip.

Leaves downy-fuzzy giving them a silvery sheen, fern-like, deeply cut and lobed both basal and on stalks, to 5″ (13 cm) long. In early spring

the basal leaves are often a beautiful wine-red before turning green.
The common name Lousewort refers to the medieval belief that plants of
the same family were a remedy for lice.
Pedicularis, Latin for "louse" or "lousy."

Pedicularis lanceolata   Swamp Wood Betony

In moist, swampy situations, restricted to the Ozark mountains. Blooms
from August to October.
Quite different from *P. canadensis.* From 1 to 3 feet (30 to 90 cm) tall,
smooth, not hairy.
Flowers terminal, cream or yellowish-white.
Leaves linear lanceolate, to 5″ (13 cm) long, with small lobes along
margins.

220

Penstemon digitalis [20]   Beard-tongue

In borders of woods, prairies, fields, along roads and railroads statewide
except northwest counties. Blooms from May to July.
The tallest of three white-flowered *Penstemon* in Missouri, to 4 feet
(1.2 m) high.
Flowers, in loose terminal clusters, are tubes with 2 upper and 3 lower
lobes. One of the 5 stamens does not produce pollen and is modified
into a hairy "tongue," probably to attract insects, thus the name Beard-
tongue.
Leaves opposite, lance-shaped, without stems, with widely spaced teeth.
Penstemon, Greek, meaning "5 stamens;" *digitalis,* Latin for "finger," referring to the Foxglove, whose botanical name is *Digitalis* and whose
much larger flowers resemble those of *Penstemon* in shape.

Penstemon pallidus   Pale Beard-tongue

In dry acid soils of glades and woods (*P. digitalis* grows in moist condi-
tions), statewide except in northwest counties. Blooms from April to
July.
Very similar to *P. digitalis* but stems and both sides of leaves are con-
spicuously hairy.
Flowers are off-white, grayish.

Penstemon tubaeflorus   Funnel-form Beard-tongue

On upland prairies, glades, in dry ground of the Ozarks and southwestern
counties. Blooms in May and June.
Flower cluster narrow.
Main leaves remain well below the inflorescence. Leaves without hair,
with broad-margined petioles.

Scrophularia marilandica [59]   Figwort, Carpenter's Square

In rich woods and woods borders, lowlands, statewide. Blooms from July
to October.

Much branched, leafy plants to 7 feet (2.1 m) tall.

Flowers are clustered terminally in open panicles in a broad inflorescence.
Individual flowers are only ⅜" (9 mm) long, sac-shaped, with a two-
lipped corolla which is green on the outside and brown-magneta inside.

Leaves lanceolate, sharply pointed, on slender petioles, opposite, with fine
teeth.

Stems 4-sided and grooved, thus the common name, Carpenter's Square.

The Family and generic name, *Scrophularia*, goes back to the medieval
"doctrine of signatures" which postulated that an imagined likeness
between parts of plants and parts of the human body was a divine
manifestation, or signature, of medicinal properties inherent in the
plant to heal the similarly shaped part of the human anatomy. The
fleshy knobs on the rhizomes were supposed to heal scrofula, a con-
stitutional disorder of a tuberculous nature. Figwort was once fig-wart,
a growth which the plants were hoped to remedy.

221

Verbascum thapsus [43]   Mullein, Flannel Plant

In dry fields, waste ground, along roads and railroads statewide. Blooms
from late May to September. Native of Europe.

This conspicuous immigrant takes over land which has been disturbed
or neglected. The flower stalk reaches to 7 feet (2.1 m).

Flowers at the end of the stalk in a tight, elongated cluster, light yellow,
5-lobed, sweet scented with 5 stamens. Each flower is about ¾" (20
mm) across.

Basal leaves, often 12" (30 cm) long, are formed during the first year.
They are oblong, tapering at the base into winged stems. The flowering
stalk, produced in the second year, is densely covered with leaves
which are smaller and upright growing.

The entire plant has a grey look because leaves and stems are covered
with dense, fine hair—thus Flannel Plant.

Verbascum, the classical Latin name for Mullein, used by Pliny; *thapsus*,
the Latin name for a plant yielding a yellow dye.

Verbascum blattaria [15]   Moth Mullein

In pastures, fields, waste ground, along roads and railroads, in the eastern,
southern, and central parts of the state. Blooms from May to September.

To 4 feet tall, either a single stem or many-branched. The branches spreading stiffly at the same angle like a partially open umbrella.

Flowers spaced in loose spikes, only a few opening at one time, are either white or lemon yellow, about ¾″ (18 mm) across, with 5 lobes and 5 stamens. The stamens are covered with violet hair. With some imagination one can see a moth's head in the flower.

Leaves are smooth, lance-shaped, with a flattened base, stemless, arranged in a spiral around the stem.

Verbascum, classical Latin name for Mullein, used by Pliny; *blattaria,* Latin, from *blatta,* the "cockroach," which the plant is supposed to discourage. Another explanation of the common name is that the flowers attract moths.

222

Veronicastrum virginicum [24]   Culver's-root

In open woods, swampy prairies and meadows, along roads and railroads statewide. Blooms from June to September.

Unbranched stalks to 6 feet (1.8 m) tall.

Flowers in spikes which emerge from a common axil, the center spike somewhat longer. The individual white flowers are tiny.

From 3 to 9 leaves to 6″ (15 cm) long in whorls spaced along the stalk. They are short stemmed, narrow lanceolate, toothed.

Veronicastrum, Latin, for Veronica and Aster. The flowers of *Veronicastrum* are very similar to those of the *Veronica* genus which, in turn, is named after Ste. Veronica. Culver's-root has medicinal applications and is named after a Dr. Coulvert, an American physician of the 17th and 18th centuries.

TRUMPET CREEPER FAMILY *Bignoniaceae*

Campsis radicans [67] Trumpet Creeper, Trumpet Vine, Devil's Shoe Laces, Shoe Strings, Hell Vine, Cow-itch

In thickets, open woods, fencerows, along roads and railroads, on waste ground statewide. Blooms from May to August.

An aggressive vine with aerial rootlets on its stems. Vines become woody with age.

Flowers in terminal clusters are tubes with 5 lobes to 3″ (80 mm) long, red or orange in color.

Compound leaves with from 7 to 11 leaflets which are opposite except the terminal one, egg-shaped and toothed, sharply pointed, to 3″ (80 mm) long.

The flowers are much visited by hummingbirds. **Some people get a Poison Ivy-type rash after touching the vine, which accounts for still another**

name, Cow-itch.

Campsis, Greek, "curved," relating to the stamens; *radicans,* Latin, "rooting," referring to the aerial rootlets.

A related vine, *Bignonia flaveolata,* Cross Vine, grows in the southeast section of Missouri. The vine is evergreen with short, orange-brown flowers in early spring.

ACANTHUS FAMILY *Acanthaceae*

Justicia americana [86]   Water Willow

On gravel and mud margins of streams, sloughs and lakes, also in ditches, statewide except northern counties. Blooms from late May to October. **223**

Much branched, shrub-like, to 3 feet (90 cm) tall. Covers extensive areas on gravel bars and muddy embankments or other wet situations.

Flowers clustered on the tip of stems which arise from the leaf axils of the upper part of the branches. Each flower is a tube nearly ¾″ (18 mm) long which opens into a notched upper and a 3-lobed lower lip. The color is pale violet.

Leaves are willow-like, narrow and opposite, stemless, 3″ to 6″ (7.5 to 15 cm) long.

Bees and other insects are much attracted by the flowers.

Justicia is named for James Justice, a Scottish botanist of the 18th century.

Ruellia strepens [70]   Wild Petunia, Smooth Ruellia

In rich lowlands or moist woods statewide. Blooms from May to October.

A perennial, either single-stemmed or branched, to 3 feet (90 cm) tall, which is either smooth or only slightly hairy.

Flowers are large tubes with 5 lobes, to 2″ (50 mm) long, Petunia-like lavender to lilac-blue, very rarely white. The flower envelope segments (calyx) are linear lanceolate, to 1″ (25 mm) long.

Leaves on short petioles, smooth, lanceolate, opposite.

Ruellia is named for Jean de la Ruelle, a French herbalist, 1474-1537; *strepens,* Latin, "rustling," a sound made by the exploding seed capsules.

Botanically, *Ruellia* is not a Petunia, which belongs to the Nightshade Family *(Solanaceae).*

Ruellia humilis   Hairy or Wild Petunia

In dry situations, statewide. Blooms from May to October.

In addition to the difference in habitat, there are three other distinguishing characteristics between this species and *R. strepens*. *R. humilis* is very hairy, a protection against drought in dry places; leaves are sessile, and calyx segments are wider and quite hairy.

PLANTAIN FAMILY *Plantaginaceae*

Plantago lanceolata [12] English Plantain, Long Plantain, Snake Plantain, Buckhorn, Rib Grass, Ripple Grass

In dry fields and pastures, lawns, waste ground, along roads and railroads statewide. Blooms from April to October. Native of Europe.

Plantains have basal rosettes of leaves from which arise the flower stalks to 15″ (38 cm) high.

Flowers are massed in narrow, terminal spikes. Though the tiny flowers are white, with a 4-parted corolla and protruding stamens, the inflorescence looks brown due to the many brown bracts which accompany the flowers.

Leaves in a basal rosette are lanceolate with parallel veins and long, tapering stems. Young leaves are eaten as "greens."

Plantago, Latin, means "foot-like," because some species have large, broad leaves; *lanceolata*, Latin, "lance-shaped," referring to the leaves.

Plantago aristata Bracted Plantain

Common statewide in almost any habitat. Blooms from May to November.
Similar to *P. lanceolata* but inflorescence enclosed by very long bracts, tipped by bristles.
Basal leaves narrow linear.

Plantago rugelii Rugel Plantain

In almost any habitat statewide. Blooms from May to October.
Inflorescence very elongated on long stalks.
Leaves broad, egg-shaped, with parallel-appearing veins.

Plantago virginica Hoary Plantain

In almost any habitat statewide. Blooms from April to June.
Much smaller than above plantains and very hairy.
Leaves egg-shaped.

Plantago pusilla Slender Plantain

On acid soils, rock outcroppings, glades, south of the Missouri River and in north-central counties. Blooms from April to June.

A miniature Plantain, to 6″ (15 cm) tall, which covers large areas. Leaves linear.

MADDER FAMILY *Rubiaceae*

Cephalanthus occidentalis [25]   Buttonbush

On borders of sloughs, lakes, rivers, river bottoms statewide. Blooms from June to September.

A large shrub, occasionally a small tree.

Flowers in ball-shaped clusters terminally on the branches. The tiny white flowers are 5-lobed, tubular, with protruding styles—the female part of the blossom. The flower clusters emerge from the leaf axils.

Leaves opposite, oblong elliptical, pointed, to 6″ (15 cm) long.

The seeds remain in spherical masses on the bushes for some time, creating the picture of a "buttonbush." Ducks, especially wood ducks, and pheasants eat the seeds.

Cephalanthus, Greek, "head [shaped] flower;" *occidentalis,* Latin, "of the West."

225

Houstonia minima [79]   Least Bluets

In prairies, pastures, glades, floodplains, rocky ledges and bluff escarpments in central and southern Missouri. Blooms from January to April.

Forms mats and colonies, not over 4″ (10 cm) high.

Flowers emerge on slender stems from axils of opposite leaves. The tiny blossoms, about ¼″ (6 mm) across, have four pointed lobes, look always skyward, and are either purple or deep violet-purple, and sometimes white, with a yellow throat.

Leaves are both basal and on the stems. The basal leaves are oval with relatively long stems, those along the stalks are narrow and without stems (sessile).

Houstonia is named for the British botanist Dr. Wm. Houston who lived in the early 18th century; *minima,* Latin, "very tiny."

Some botanists prefer the name *Hedyotis* to *Houstonia.*

No other plant can better exemplify the possible confusion created by the use of common names. *Houstonia* is called: Quaker Ladies, Quaker Bonnets, Star Violet, Little Washerwoman, Blue-eyed Babies, Wild Forget-me-not, Eye-bright, Angel Eyes, Nuns, Innocents, Star of Bethlehem, Venus' Pride, and, of course, Bluets.

Houstonia pusilla   Star Violet

In acid soils on glades and rocky ledges, in dry, open places in the eastern

Ozarks. Blooms in March and April.
Even smaller than *H. minima* with deep lavender or purple flowers.

Houstonia caerulea   Bluets, Eye-bright

In acid soil on moist ledges of sandstone and granite, in swampy meadows,
low prairies, sandy open woods and glades of the eastern Ozarks.
Blooms in April and May.
Slightly taller than the two preceding species, with light blue flowers.

Houstonia longifolia [10]   Long-leaved Houstonia

226

In rocky, open woods, prairies, glades, usually in acid soils in the Ozark
region north to the Missouri River. Blooms from April to July.
Upright, slender and branching stalks, usually 8″ (20 cm) high but sometimes taller, arising from a basal rosette of leaves.
White, 4-lobed flowers are carried on slender stems arising from upper leaf
axils. The calyx, the flower part from which the flower-tube emerges,
is quite large.
Leaves are of two kinds. The basal leaves form a rosette, have short
stems, and are oblong, pointed. Those along the stems are opposite,
quite narrow, and pointed at both ends. Both types have only one
central vein. A very rare variety has grass-like leaves.
Houstonia is named for the British botanist, Dr. Wm. Houston, who lived
in the early 18th century; *longifolia*, Latin, "long-leaved." It is also
known as *Hedyotis longifolia*.

HONEYSUCKLE FAMILY   *Caprifoliaceae*

Lonicera flava [32]   Yellow Honeysuckle

In rocky woods, ledges, along streams in the Ozark region. Blooms in April
and May.
A woody, trailing or climbing, or sometimes almost shrub-like Honeysuckle.
Flowers are 1″ (25 mm) long tubes with protruding stamens carried in
terminal clusters above a platter-like union of two jointed leaves which
clasp the stem. Colors are orange or orange-yellow.
Leaves opposite, without stems (sessile), thick, egg-shaped, with a grey
underside.
Fruit is a berry esteemed by birds, as are those of other Honeysuckle
species.

Lonicera is named after Adam Lonitzer, a German physician and naturalist of the 16th century; *flava*, Latin, "yellow."

Lonicera sempervirens   Trumpet Honeysuckle

Along roadsides, sandy or rocky stream banks, and in thickets in central and southern counties. Escaped from cultivation. Blooms from April to July.

Flowers deep scarlet or yellow-orange.

Leaves paddle-shaped, rounded, opposite.

Lonicera japonica   Japanese Honeysuckle

In fence rows, open woods, rocky slopes, ditches, roadsides and railroads, **227** scattered in southern and central counties. Escaped from cultivation. Blooms in May and June. Native of Asia.

A strong climber which strangles shrubs and trees in its path, covers large areas—a very serious pest.

Flowers reddish on the outside, yellowish inside.

Lonicera prolifera   Grape Honeysuckle

In open woods, on bluffs, wooded thickets, in the northern two-thirds of the state. Blooms from April to June.

Flowers usually pale yellow.

Leaves paddle-shaped, the uppermost ones are joined in a circle around the stems and often have a white coating.

Sambucus canadensis [16]   American Elderberry, Common Elderberry, Common Elder

In open woods, fencerows, along streams, roads and railroads statewide. Blooms from late May to July.

Shrub, rarely a small tree, to 10 feet (3 m) high, thicket-forming. Stems smooth, pale grey-brown, pithy inside.

Flowers very small, white, with 5 petals and 5 stamens. The inflorescence is an umbrella-shaped open cluster, carried terminally, delicately scented.

Leaves are opposite, pinnately compound. Leaflets are elliptical to lance-shaped, from 3″ to 6″ (7.5 to 15 cm) long, and finely toothed. The lower leaflets are sometimes 3-divided.

Fruits are purple-black, berry-like and juicy. They are used for jellies, wine-making and pies. Animals and birds are attracted to this delicacy. Unripe fruits can be eaten like capers.

Sambucus is the classical Latin name for Elder.

Triosteum perfoliatum [59]   Common Horse Gentian, Wild Coffee, Tinker's Weed

In dry, open woods statewide except southeast lowlands. Blooms from May to July.

Leafy, upright stalk to 4 feet (1.2 m) tall.

Flowers, clustered on very short stems in leaf axils, are reddish-brown and almost hidden by a green calyx. The flowers are tube-shaped with 5 small lobes.

Leaves are opposite and joined around the stalk (connate), to 5″ (13 cm) long, broad lanceolate with smooth margins.

Seeds look like little oranges and remain through late summer and fall on the stalks.

Triosteum, Greek, shortened by Linneaus from *triosteo* and *spermum* meaning "3 stony seeds;" *perfoliatum,* Latin, means "going through the leaf," the appearance of the stalk.

228

Triosteum aurantiacum   Scarlet-fruited Horse Gentian

In rich woods, absent from western and southeastern counties. Blooms from May to July.

Very similar to *T. perfoliatum* but leaves are on stems (petioles), opposite, and not joined around the stem.

Viburnum rufidulum [9]   Southern Black Haw

In dry woods, rich valleys, along streams, absent from northern counties. Blooms in April and May.

A shrub, but frequently a small tree, to a maximum of 20 feet (6 m) tall.

Flowers are white, in large clusters to 5″ (13 cm) across, borne terminally with individual flowers only ¼″ (6 mm) wide, 5-lobed.

Leaves are shiny glossy, opposite, on leaf stalks covered by dense red hair, leathery and thick, either egg or oval shaped, dark green above, lighter with rust-colored hair underneath.

Fruit a dark blue drupe (a stone fruit surrounded by soft tissue, as in a plum) with a bloom, much esteemed by animals and birds.

Viburnum, classical Latin name of unknown meaning; *rufidulum,* Latin, "somewhat reddish."

Viburnum prunifolium   Black Haw

In dry woods, rich valleys, along streams statewide. Blooms in April and May.

Flowers similar to V. *rufidulum.*
Leaves drawn out to a point, finely toothed, not shiny, yellowish-green.
Twigs not hairy.
Fruit a dark blue drupe.

Viburnum rafinesquianum [15] Arrow-wood, Missouri Viburnum, Downy Arrow-wood

On wooded bluffs, rocky open woods, along streams, missing from southeast, east-central, and western counties. Blooms in May and June.
A small shrub, often as understory in woods, to 10 feet (3 m) high.
Flowers white, very small, in domed terminal clusters up to 4″ (10 cm) across.
Leaves opposite, ovate, long-pointed, with from 4 to 10 coarse teeth on each margin. Fall coloration dull purple-red to dull wine-purple. This species is recommended for home plantings.
Fruit a blue-black drupe.
Viburnum, classical Latin name of unknown meaning; *rafinesquianum* for Samuel Constantine Rafinesque Schmaltz, 1783-1840, a botanist who spent some years in the United States.

229

TEASEL FAMILY *Dipsacaceae*

Dipsacus sylvestris [72] Teasel

In fields, pastures, waste ground, along roads and railroads in southern and central Missouri. Blooms from June to October. Native of Europe.
Stout prickly stems with many branches, to 8 feet (2.4 m) tall.
Tiny flowers, massed in a tight cylindrical head, each with a tubular corolla, in lilac or pink-purple. These flower heads are interspersed with prickly bristles, and spine-tipped slender bracts are conspicuous surrounding the inflorescence.
Leaves from 6″ to 12″ (15 to 30 cm) long, lance-shaped, without stems, opposite. Upper pair of leaves are without stems and are joined around the stalk.
A closely related Teasel, *D. fullonum,* was cultivated and the dried fruiting heads put on spindles to raise the nap of woolen cloth.
Dipsacus, Greek, means "to thirst," a reference to the leaf arrangement of many members of the Teasel Family that have leaves joined together around the stalks which act as catch-basins for water; *sylvestris,* Latin, "of the woods," though our Teasel never grows in woods.

BELLFLOWER FAMILY *Campanulaceae*

Campanula americana [89]   Tall Bellflower, Bluebell

Along streams, in stream bottomlands, borders of woods, variable habitat statewide. Blooms from June to October.

Straight stalks with many branches to 6 feet (1.8 m) and higher.

Flowers of this species are not bell-shaped but are 5-pointed stars slightly over 1″ (25 mm) across. At the inner center is a white ring and a very long pistil, 4-lobed. Its end protrudes prominently. Flowers emerge from narrow green bracts along the stalk and branches. They are violet-blue, sometimes whitish, rarely white. The flowering habit is unusual in that blossoms may be open without apparent sequence along the stalks.

230

Leaves 3″ to 6″ (7.5 to 15 cm) long, lance-shaped, stemless or with very short stems. A plant of creek beds which self-seeds profusely in gardens.

Campanula, Latin, "little bell."

Lobelia spicata [17]   Spiked Lobelia

In rocky, open woods, fields, along streams, sloughs, ponds, statewide. Blooms from May to August.

Single stalks from 1 to 3 feet (30 to 90 cm) tall.

Flowers in a terminal spike, as the name of the plant indicates. Individual blossoms are only ⅜″ (8 mm) long with 2 lips, the upper 2-divided, the lower with 3 lobes. Color pale blue or whitish. Each flower is accompanied by a small, slender leaf.

Lower leaves are alternate, oblong or lanceolate, slightly toothed, to 3½″ (9 cm) long. Leaves higher up on the stalk become progressively narrower and smaller.

Lobelia is named after the 16th century Flemish herbalist, Mathias von Lobel; *spicata*, Latin, "with a spike."

Lobelia inflata   Indian Tobacco

In woods, fields, bottomlands statewide. Blooms from June to October.

To 3 feet (90 cm) tall.

Flowers on upper part of stalk, each subtended by a small leaf, pale violet to white. Ovaries become inflated as seeds ripen.

Leaves usually toothed, hairy, oblong, to 2½″ (65 mm) long.

Plant contains a narcotic poison.

Lobelia siphilitica [90] Blue or Great Lobelia

In wet areas, along streams, in ditches, low wet woods, statewide. Blooms
from August to October.
Unbranched stalks to 3 feet (90 cm) tall.
Flowers grow from leaf axils of upper leaves. They have the typical Lobelia shape—a tube with a 2-parted upper and 3-lobed lower lip. Individual blossoms to 1″ (25 mm) long in a great range of colors—light
blue-violet or dark blue, purple, lavender, rarely white.
Leaves alternate, light green, narrowly lance-shaped with fine teeth widely
spaced, or no teeth at all, their length from 2″ to 6″ (5 to 15 cm).
Plants contain a narcotic poison and were formerly used medicinally. In
18th century Europe it was believed that the plant contained a remedy
for venereal disease, thus the botanical species name.
Lobelia, named for the 16th century herbalist Matthias von Lobel (also
known as de l'Obel).

231

Lobelia cardinalis [75] Cardinal Flower

On margins of streams, sloughs, springs, low wet areas of south and central
Missouri, scattered in the north. Blooms from July to October.
Stalks usually unbranched, about 3 feet (90 cm) tall, but sometimes taller.
Flowers in dense terminal spikes. Like other Lobelia flowers the corolla
tube has a 2-parted upper and a 3-divided lower lip, is nearly 1½″ (38
mm) long with a bundle of stamens protruding. Color is cardinal red,
rarely vermillion, and extremely rarely white.
Leaves are alternate, numerous, dark green, 2″ to 6″ (5 to 15 cm) long,
lance-shaped, finely toothed.
Lobelia, named after the 16th century Flemish herbalist Matthias von
Lobel (also known as de l'Obel); *cardinalis,* Latin, "of a cardinal," for
the cardinal-red flowers.

Specularia perfoliata [82] Venus' Looking Glass

On prairies, waste ground, fields, open woods, along streams statewide.
Blooms from April to August.
Usually a single-stalked plant to 18″ (45 cm) tall.
Flowers, surrounded by slender leaf-like bracts, emerge from the leaf
axils. They are star shaped, about ½″ (12 mm) across, blue-purple,
rarely white. Flowers on the lower parts of the stalk never open but
produce seeds.
Toothed leaves are round with a base which clasps the stem.
Specularia, Latin, "looking glass" or "mirror;" *perfoliata,* Latin, "going
through the leaf," referring to the stalk.

COMPOSITE FAMILY *Asteraceae (Compositae)*

The Composite Family, by far the largest family in Missouri—though it is second to the Orchids worldwide—can be grouped into three major divisions based on flower head arrangement: ray flowers only—the *Liguliflorae* of botany; disk flowers only, no ray flowers; and both ray and disk flowers present.

232

RAY FLOWERS ONLY

Cichorium intybus [88] Chicory, Succory, Blue Sailors, Coffee Weed

In fields, pastures, waste ground, roadsides, statewide except southeast lowlands. Blooms from May to October. Native of Europe.

Stiff, angular branches are characteristic of this common roadside weed. Shrub-like, to 3 feet (90 cm) tall.

Flower heads emerge all along the stems. The ray flowers are light blue, rarely white, strap-shaped and toothed at the end. They are actually tubes which are split open.

Leaves resemble Dandelion leaves with their prominent center vein, deep lobes, and often spines. Leaves on upper branches may be entire, without stem, and narrow.

The roots have been used here and in Europe as an additive, or maybe an adulterant, in coffee, especially in Austria.

Cichorium, adaptation of an Arabian word for coffee, as is Chicory; *intybus* is the Latin name for the plant. According to the Roman Pliny, *Cichorium* is the ancient Egyptian name of the plant.

Hieracium gronovii [41] Hawkweed

Rocky, dry open woods, fields, ravines, in eastern, central, and southern counties. Blooms from May to October.

A hairy plant of variable height, from 12″ to over 2½ feet (30 to 75 cm).

Flower heads in open clusters on terminals of stems, small, about ½″ across (12 mm), yellow. The tiny ray flowers are squared with notched tips.

Leaves are hairy, oblong to lance-shaped.

Hieracium, Greek, the name of a plant named for a hawk; *gronovii,* for Jan Henry Gronovius, 1794-1830.

Krigia biflora [38]   Dwarf Dandelion

In open woods, along streams, fields and meadows, generally south of the Missouri River. Blooms from May to August.

Plants to 2 feet (60 cm) tall, normally with a clasping leaf midway on the flower stalk.

Flowers are Dandelion-like, orange-yellow, to 1½" (40 mm) across at the tips of the stems which emerge and fork from a clasping leaf.

Basal leaves with blunted tips to 6" (15 cm) long may vary in shape from oblong to pointed lance-shaped, may or may not have lobes, and may have a few teeth or none.

Krigia for David Krieg, a German plant collector in the American colonies; *biflora,* Latin, "two-flowered," though the species frequently has many more than two flowers on a plant.

Krigia dandelion   Potato Dandelion

On acid soils of prairies, rocky glades, roadsides, south of the Missouri River. Blooms from April to June.

The flowerstalk, usually 12" (30 cm) high, is not hollow nor with the milky juice of Dandelion.

A handsome, dandelion-like flowerhead of a bright yellow color.

Leaves basal only, narrow, with a few teeth or lobes, to 6" (15 cm) long.

Root bears potato-like tubers.

Krigia virginica   Carolina Dwarf Dandelion

Usually on acid ground, on rocks, prairies, meadows, south of the Missouri River and in east-central counties. Blooms from April to August.

Truly a miniature Dandelion, rarely over 6" (15 cm) high.

Leaves basal, not over 4" (10 cm) long, Dandelion-like.

Forms large colonies and completely fills the cracks in rocks.

Lactuca floridana [90]   False Lettuce

On waste ground, wooded slopes, along streams, roads and railroads statewide. Blooms from August to October.

One of seven Lettuce species in Missouri, grows as a leafy plant to 8 feet (2.4 m) high.

Flower heads in spreading panicles with up to 17 florets in each. The bluish, sometimes nearly white, ray flowers open a few at one time on each panicle.

233

Leaves are large and variable, triangular or deeply indented, almost to the midrib. The margins are broadly scalloped.

After the flowers have bloomed and fallen off there remain tufts of white bristles, tightly bunched, for a long time.

The green parts contain a milky juice.

Lactuca, Latin from *lacta,* "milk."

Lactuca scariola   Prickly Lettuce

In waste areas, fields, roadsides, statewide. Blooms from June to October.

A very tall weed from Europe, often 7 feet (2.1 m) or higher.

Many small flowerheads with yellowish strap-florets which turn bluish on drying.

Leaves entire, spade-shaped or, more often, deeply lobed, clasping the stem, with many short, weak spines.

The green parts of the plant contain the typical white sap of the Lettuce family.

Lactuca canadensis   Wild Lettuce

In borders of woods, fields, mud banks, gravel bars, statewide. Blooms from July to September.

Appearance and flowers much like *L. scariola* but leaves have no prickles and do not clasp the stalk. The lower leaves are deeply lobed, the higher ones are narrow, lance-shaped. Both are sessile.

Pyrrhopappus carolinianus [38]   False Dandelion

In fields, dry or wet situations, roadsides, waste places, statewide. Blooms from May to October.

Depending on soil and moisture, this member of the Composite sub-family *Ligulaceae*—those with strap-like florets—may be found flowering when hardly 12″ (30 cm) tall, but may reach 4½ feet (1.4 m) in rich bottomlands.

Flowerheads are characteristically sulphur yellow, otherwise exactly like Dandelion. Each flowerhead lasts only from 1 to 2 days.

Leaves of two kinds. A basal rosette with deeply lobed feather-like and toothed leaves which can reach a length of 10″ (25 cm); some teeth recurve. By flowering time the basal leaves have totally or mostly disappeared. Leaves on stems are few—never more than 6 per stem—toothed or narrow lanceolate and partly clasping, without stems.

Pyrrhopappus, from Greek *pyr,* "fire," and *pappus,* the botanical name for the bristles or hair emerging from the seed covers (achene) of the Composite Family florets, which in this species are rusty or brick-red.

234

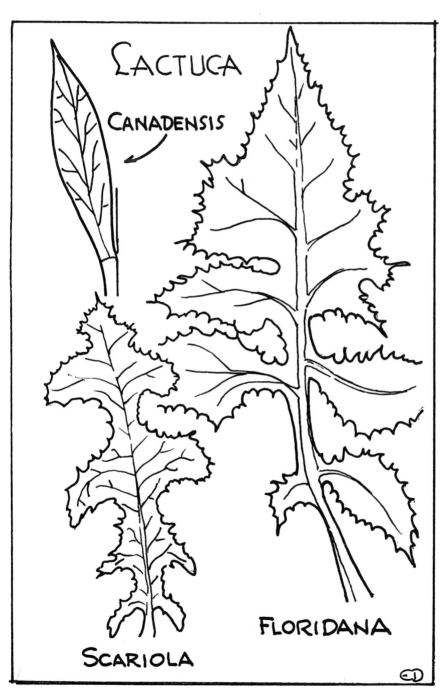

LACTUCA

CANADENSIS

SCARIOLA

FLORIDANA

235

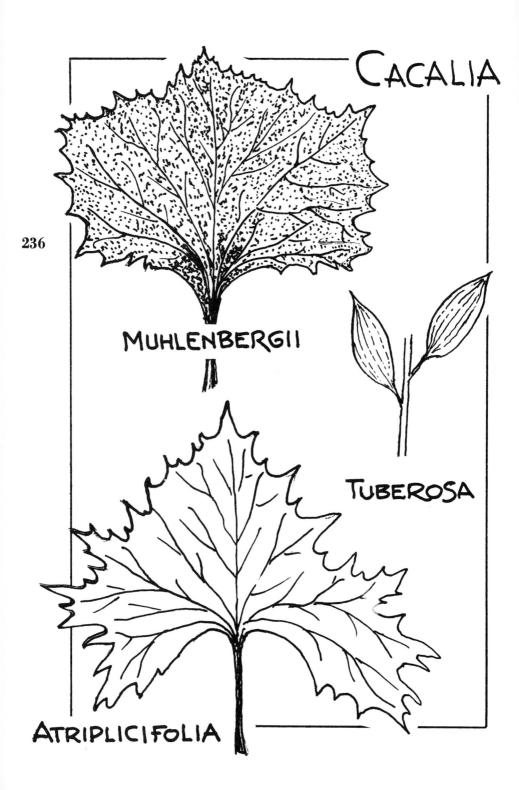

CACALIA

236

MUHLENBERGII

TUBEROSA

ATRIPLICIFOLIA

Pyrrhopappus exists both as an annual and a winter annual. In the latter case it produces leaves during one year and flowers the next.

Tragopogon dubius [37]   Goat's Beard

In fields, meadows, waste ground, along roads and railroads, statewide. Blooms from May to July. Native of Europe.

Fleshy stalks, usually single but sometimes several, to 2½ feet (76 cm) tall. Flowerheads on stalks which show a distinct thickening below the inflorescence. Flowers yellow, Dandelion-like, but larger. Bracts longer than ray flowers, which appear straplike. Flowers open in the morning and close by noon when the sun shines.

Leaves, both basal and along stems, are narrow linear, alternate and clasp the stem.

237

Seed-heads much like those of Dandelion but much larger and handsome.

Trapogopgon, Greek, "goat's beard," referring to the seed-head; *dubius*, Latin, means "doubtful," because the plant had been for years mistaken for another species.

Tragopogon porrifolius   Salsify or Oyster Plant

On waste ground, roadsides, until recently very restricted, but now spreading along highways in central counties. Blooms from May to July. Native of Europe.

A handsome immigrant with purple flowerheads on leafy stems to 3 feet (90 cm) tall.

With the exception of the color, there is no apparent difference from *T. dubius*.

The roots of selected and improved plants are cultivated for the vegetable Salsify.

DISK FLOWERS ONLY

Antennaria plantaginifolia [5]   Pussy's Toes, Ladies' Tobacco, Everlasting, Indian Tobacco

On dry and rocky slopes in acid soils statewide. Blooms from April to June. Whitish, densely woolly plants with flower stalks to 10″ (25 cm) high. "Flowers" are actually clusters of flowers. The plant is dioecious, meaning that male and female flowers are produced by different plants. The male flowerheads are on shorter stalks with smaller flowers, showing purple or dark brown anthers. The fuzzy flowerheads give the plant

the name Pussy's Toes. They are off-white, often turning light pink.
Leaves are of two kinds. Basal leaves are paddle-shaped with long stems and 3 prominent ribs. Those along the stalk are narrow, pointed, without stems. The plantain-leaf-shaped basal leaves are usually not yet developed when the plant is in flower.
Antennaria, Latin, "with antennas," referring to the bristle-like hairs protruding from the flowerheads resembling the antennas of butterflies; *plantaginifolia*, Latin, "with leaves like a Plantain."

Antennaria neglecta   Field Cat's-foot or Pussy's Toes

238

In fields, prairies, open woods of north and west Missouri. Blooms from April to June.
Much like *A. plantaginifolia*, but leaves are quite narrow with only one central vein.

Cacalia atriplicifolia [25]   Pale Indian Plantain (see p. 236)

In low and upland woods, ravines, along railroads, statewide. Blooms from June to October.
A stout single stem with a silvery coating which can be rubbed off, to 5 feet (1.5 m) tall, having widely spaced leaves and crowned by a flower cluster.
Flowerheads, consisting of a few tubular florets, numerous, cylindrical. The whitish disk florets (no ray florets) surrounded by long, stiff green bracts. The many flowerheads arranged in a flat-topped, loose compound, a corymb.
Leaves stand out from the main stem on long petioles at an oblique angle. They are irregularly fan-shaped with angular lobes, the lower ones wider than long, to 6″ (15 cm) wide.
Cacalia is an ancient name of uncertain meaning; *atriplicifolia*, Latin, "with a leaf of *Atriplex*," the Saltbush.

Cacalia muhlenbergii   Great Indian Plantain (see p. 236)

In rich woods on north and east-facing slopes, absent from the western one-third of the state. Blooms from May to September.
Similar to *C. atriplicifolia* but without silvery coating and lower leaves kidney-shaped with many serrations.

Cacalia tuberosa   Indian Plantain (see p. 236)

On glades and prairies, the only *Cacalia* not growing in woods, absent from northern counties and the southeast lowlands. Blooms from May to August.

Flower stalk to 3 feet (90 cm) tall.
Look for large, toothless, oval lower leaves with main veins running parallel.

Carduus nutans [73]   Musk Thistle, Nodding Thistle

In waste places, along roads and railways, spreading statewide. Blooms from June to October. Native of Europe.

Plants are from 2 to 6 feet (.6 to 1.8 m) tall.

Flowerheads, composed of hundreds of disk florets, are rose-purple, to 2½″ (65 mm) across, supported by pointed and recurved bracts. Mature flowerheads take on a nodding stance.

Leaves are of two kinds. Those of the basal rosette are long, deeply incised, very spiny, with a prominent, nearly white midrib. These basal leaves have disappeared by flowering time. Narrower, deeply incised, spiny leaves emerge from the stems. The stems themselves are prickly, winged.

This immigrant arrived in the U.S. early in the 20th century. A single plant can produce up to 10,000 seeds which are supplied with parachutes for wind-borne dissemination. The thistle is spreading rapidly, mainly along roads, all over the state.

C. nutans lives either as an annual, completing its life cycle in one season, or a winter annual, a term used for plants which form leaf growth during one year and go into flowering during the following growing season.

Carduus is the classical Roman name for thistle; *nutans*, Latin, means "nodding."

239

Centaurea cyanus [87]   Cornflower

In fields, waste ground, roadsides, scattered statewide. Blooms from May to September. Native of Europe.

An annual garden plant, often escaped, to 3 feet (90 cm) tall and much branched. On rare occasions it will cover entire abandoned fields.

Flowerheads about 1″ (25 mm) across, the ray flowers arising from a vase-shaped involucre. Colors clear blue or pink or whitish.

Leaves narrow linear, sharply pointed, alternate.

Cornflower got its name in Europe where Corn (Korn) means wheat or oats, and where *Centaurea* is a common weed in grain fields. The name has nothing to do with our Corn.

Centaurea, named after the centaur Chiron who was a healer; *cyanus*, Greek, "blue."

Cirsium vulgare [73]   Bull Thistle

In fields, waste ground, roadsides statewide. Blooms from June to September. Native of Europe.

A very tall, much branched Thistle, often over 7 feet (2.1 m) tall. Upper part of stems and branches are winged with a wavy, prickly tissue.

Flowerheads are typical thistles, with a prominent involucre, the mass of bracts. Bracts are covered with a fine, cobweb-like silk. Color of flowers is a pale lavender or rose-lavender.

Leaves deeply cleft into spiny divisions, their upper surface with stiff bristles.

240   One identification mark of the Bull Thistle is that the spines grow along the stems right up to the flowerheads.

Cirsium, Latin, means "swelled vein" as thistles were supposed to help this problem; *vulgare*, Latin, "common."

Cirsium altissimum   Tall Thistle

On slopes, in bottomlands, along roadsides, statewide. Blooms from July to October.

This is a tall native Thistle which can reach 10 feet (over 3 m) or more.

Flowerheads are many, rose-purple or magenta, rarely white. Outer involucre bracts have a dark glandular spot while all bracts have a weak prickle.

Leaves ovate-lanceolate, not deeply incised, with slender or shallow-broad teeth. The underside of the leaves is woolly hairy.

Elephantopus carolinianus [28]   Elephant's Foot

In wooded valleys, lowlands, openings in woods, south of the Missouri River. Blooms from August to October.

Usually a much forked plant with angular branches to nearly 3 feet (90 cm) tall.

Flowers are actually flowerheads, each with only 2 to 5 florets. The light lavender to whitish flowerheads are bunched in a flat cluster, called a glomerule, and this is surrounded by large, leaf-like bracts. This odd arrangement makes *Elephantopus* an unusual member of the Composite Family.

Leaves, scattered along the stems, are alternate, oval, obliquely toothed, the lower ones narrowed rather abruptly at their base, the upper ones generally without stems (petioles) and quite small.

Elephantopus, Greek, "elephant foot," is a translation of an aboriginal name which does not explain anything. The genus *Elephantopus* is found primarily in the tropics and warm regions of the world.

Eupatorium rugosum [26]   White Snakeroot

In rich or rocky woods, base of bluffs, clearings, statewide. Blooms from
July to October.

Upright perennial plants to 4 feet (1.2 m) tall, much branched.

Flowerheads in loose, flat-topped clusters at the end of branches. Flowers
point upward, are clear white, and give the impression of tufts. Each
flowerhead contains up to 24 individual tubular florets. Bracts of involucre are acutely pointed and without hair.

Leaves are opposite, thin, on long stems, lanceolate to egg-shaped, narrowing at the base, with coarse teeth.

**This plant is the cause of "milk-sickness," as it poisons cattle and killed
many early settlers who drank the poisoned milk, including Abraham
Lincoln's mother.**

Eupatorium is named for Eupater, "good father," Mithidates, an ancient
Greek healer who used some *Eupatorium* species in his trade; *rugosum*,
Latin, "wrinkled," reason unknown.

241

Eupatorium altissimum [28]   Tall Thoroughwort

In prairies, fields, open woods, waste ground, statewide but rare in the
southeast lowlands. Blooms from August to October.

An upright plant to 5 feet (1.5 m) tall.

Many flower clusters arise on stems near top of stalk forming a loose,
domed mass of bloom. The individual flowerheads are drab, whitish
to grey-white.

Leaves are narrow and toothed. Those on the flower stems very small and
short, those along the stalk to 5″ (13 cm) long. They are without
stems and opposite.

Eupatorium is named for the ancient Greek Eupater, "good father,"
Mithidates, who used some *Eupatorium* species for healing; *altissimum*,
Latin, "the highest."

Eupatorium serotinum   Late Boneset

In fields, waste places, roadsides, near moisture, statewide. Blooms from
August to October.

Very similar to *E. rugosum* but inflorescence spreads wider and looks defi-
nitely gray. The flowerheads hold up to 15 florets. Bracts of involucre
are broadly rounded and densely hairy.

Leaves are on longer stalks, coarsely toothed, opposite.

Eupatorium perfoliatum   Boneset

In moist situations statewide. Blooms from July to October.

Flowerheads white, inflorescence flat-topped
Opposite leaves are joined around the stem.
Stems conspicuously hairy.

Eupatorium sessilifolium   Upland Boneset

In dry rocky woods, bluffs, on the banks of streams, scattered statewide
except for western counties. Blooms from July to September.
Flower clusters white, on stalks to 6 feet (1.8 m) tall.
Leaves opposite and sessile or with very short stalks, sharply toothed. The
base of the smooth leaves is rounded, somewhat heart-shaped.

242

Eupatorium purpureum   Green-stemmed Joe-Pye-weed

On slopes and low, wet ground statewide. Blooms from July to September.
To 6 feet (1.8 m) tall.
Flowerheads in domed convex clusters, usually dull pink to pale pink-
purplish, sometimes creamy white, with only 3-5 florets in each in-
florescence.
Leaves in whorls on stalks, lanceolate, toothed, sharply narrowed toward
base.
Stems are green with purplish areas where leaves emerge.

Eupatorium coelestinum [90]   Mist Flower, Wild Ageratum, Blue Boneset

In moist places, ditches, low places, south of the Missouri River. Blooms
from July to October.
Grows in dense stands to about 2½ feet (76 cm) tall, but normally much
lower.
Flowerheads in terminal flat clusters of blue or blue-violet "heads," each
with from 30 to 70 flowers.
Leaves opposite, toothed, somewhat triangular (truncate).
This showy perennial resembles the annual *Ageratum* of gardens. It forms
a dense and spreading root-mass and will take over in gardens unless
restrained.
The name *Eupatorium* from Eupater Mithridates, a healer; *coelestinum*,
Latin, means "sky-blue." A white variety exists but has not yet been
reported from Missouri.

Liatris aspera [77] *(scariosa)*   Blazing Star, Gay Feather

In dry upland prairies, glades, open woods, along roads and railroads,
statewide except southeast lowlands. Blooms from August to November.

EUPATORIUM

SESSILIFOLIUM

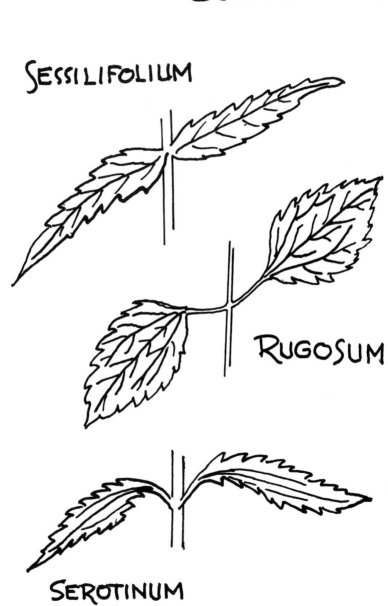

RUGOSUM

SEROTINUM

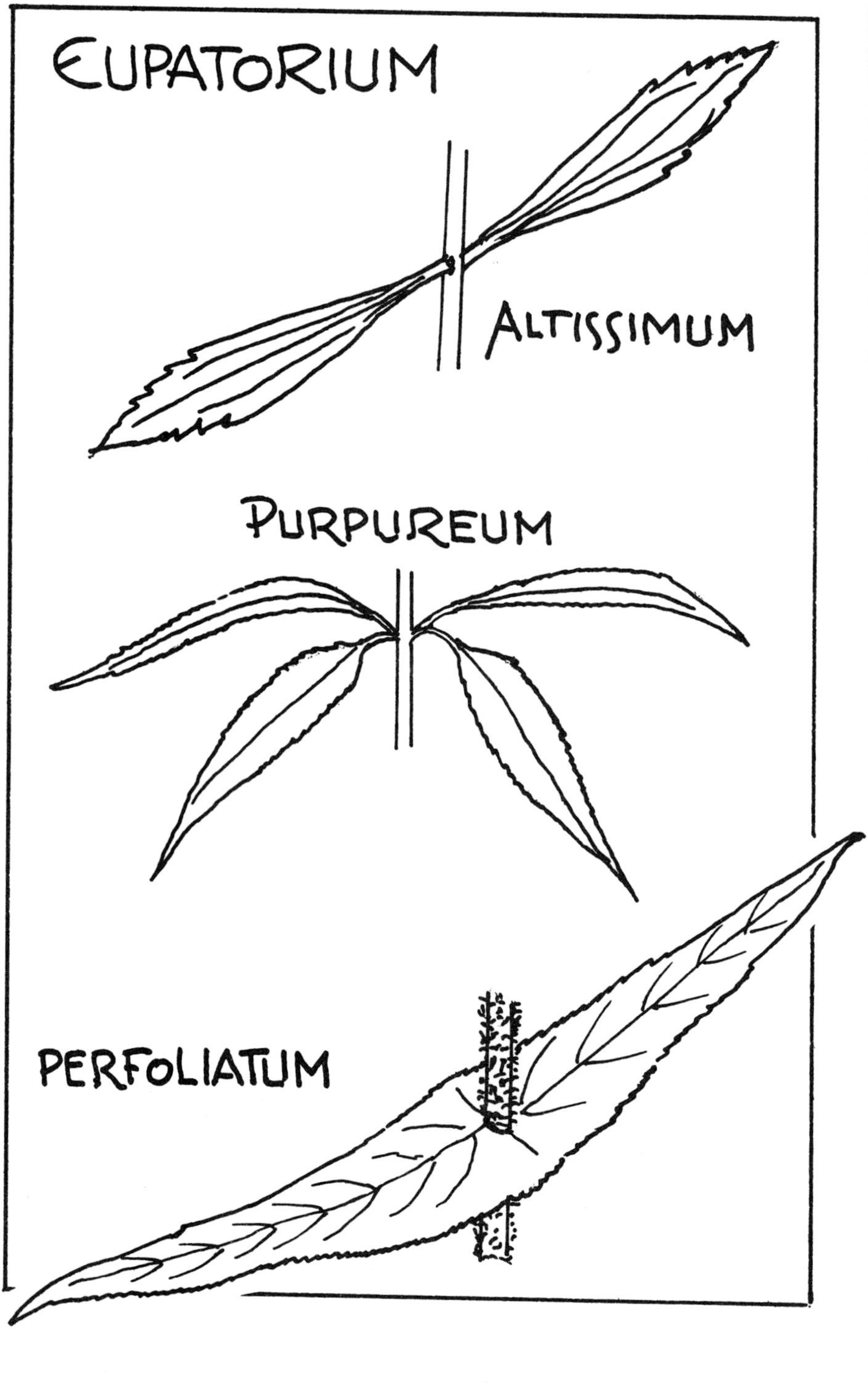

EUPATORIUM

244

ALTISSIMUM

PURPUREUM

PERFOLIATUM

Unbranched stalks, usually 2 to 3 feet (60 to 90 cm) tall, but to 5 feet (1.5 m) under favorable conditions.

Flowerheads in terminal spikes, arising from leaf axils, each head bowl-shaped, surrounded by bracts. The lower bracts with broadly rounded tips, all spreading outward. Flowerheads are to 1″ (25 mm) across, hold up to 60 individual flowers, and their color varies from magenta to rose-purple or pale violet; white specimens are rare.

Leaves are alternate and dense around the stalk, narrow lance-shaped, to 12″ (30 cm) long at base of plant but much shorter toward the top. Stem and leaves hairy.

The root is a round corm. *Liatris* does well in gardens in full sun.

Liatris, meaning unknown; *aspera,* Latin, "rough."   **245**

Liatris pycnostachya [77]   Blazing Star, Gay Feather, Hairy Button Snakeroot

On prairies, rocky open ground, along roads and railroads statewide except southeast lowlands. Blooms from July to October.

Unbranched stalks to 5 feet (1.5 m) tall, sometimes seen by the thousands in the lowlands of southwestern Missouri.

Flowers in spikes along the upper 20″ (50 cm) of stalk, closely set with a great number of crimson, magenta flowerheads which do not possess any ray flowers. Bracts surrounding flowerheads are spreading and sometimes recurved. A rare white form exists and is sold commercially.

Leaves quite narrow, to 4″ (10 cm) long, pointing upward and growing densely around the stalk.

Root is a rounded corm. The plant does well in gardens when given full sun.

The meaning of *Liatris* is unknown; *pycnostachya,* Greek, means "thick-spiked."

Liatris squarrosa   Scaly Blazing Star

On rocky glades, bluffs, and open woods, absent from the northwest and southeast corners of the state. Blooms from June to September.

Usually only a few rose-purple flowerheads. Bracts of involucre are pointed and spreading.

Liatris cylindracea   Cylindric Blazing Star

On glades, bluffs, open woods of south and east-central Missouri. Blooms from July to September.

Flowerheads either single or few, rose-purple. Bracts of involucre in a tight cylinder, each bract with a pointed tip.

Vernonia baldwini [69]   Ironweed

In waste areas, fields, glades, along roads and railroads statewide. Blooms
   from May to September.
Single stalks to 4 feet (1.2 m) tall.
Flowerheads in open, flat-topped clusters carried terminally, about ½″ (12
   mm) across and contain up to 50 disk florets, surrounded by many
   bracts which form a "basket." Colors are rose-purple or magenta. This
   is the earliest flowering of five *Vernonia* species in Missouri. To many
   people the Vernonias are the most beautiful of our fall-blooming
   plants.
Leaves alternate, rough hairy, lanceolate, sharply pointed at tips and
   bases, with short stems and fine teeth.
Vernonia is named for William Vernon, an 18th century British botanist
   who travelled in North America; *baldwini* for William Baldwin, 1779-
   1819, the original collector of the plant.

246

Other *Vernonia* species:

The species listed below have many characteristics in common. In contrast to *V. baldwini* they like moist ground, even gravel bars. They
   all flower from July to September.
They are tall, to 4 feet (1.2 m), but sometimes much taller.
Flowers are purple to rose-purple. The best way to identify them is by
   observing the bracts which surround the flowerheads.

Vernonia crinata   Great Iron-weed

Found in the Ozarks south of the Missouri River.
Bracts of involucre prolonged into thread-like tips.
Leaves narrow, willow-like, finely toothed.

Vernonia missurica   Drummond's Iron-weed

Found in northern and eastern Missouri.
Inner bracts of involucre blunt.
A densely hairy plant. Leaves similar to *V. crinata* but hairy.

Vernonia altissima   Tall Iron-weed

Scattered in eastern and central Missouri.
Inner bracts of involucre blunt. Inflorescence more open than other Ver-
   nonias.
Leaves very long, fine hairy on underside only.

Liatris Bracts

ASPERA

PYCHNOSTACHIA

SQUARROSA

CYLINDRACEA

VERNONIA BRACTS

MISSURICA

BALDWINII

FASCICULATA

CRINATA

ALTISSIMA

Vernonia fasciculata   Western Iron-weed

In north and west-central counties.
Dense inflorescence with erect branches.
Similar to *V. altissima* but leaves are hairless on underside and are pitted
with dot-like depressions.

BOTH DISK AND RAY FLOWERS

Achillea millefolium [22]   Yarrow, Milfoil   249

In waste places, roadsides, fields, statewide. Blooms from May to No-
vember. Native of Eurasia.
A widely distributed and often dominant plant in the landscape with a
simple or branched stem to 2½ feet (76 cm) tall.
Flowerheads in dense, flat-topped clusters, carried terminally. Ray flowers
are tiny and white, rarely pink, while the disk is yellow.
Leaves are finely dissected, fern-like, to 10″ (25 cm) long, narrow, oblong.
Yarrow has a strong, pungent odor but is much used in Europe for sheep
fodder.
Achillea, named for the Greek hero Achilles who is said to have used the
plant to heal wounds; *millefolium,* Latin, "thousand leaves," Milfoil
is of French origin and also means "thousand leaves."

Aster

Of the 29 species of Aster found in Missouri, 20 have a wide distribution. Three species have been selected as typical.

Aster novae-angliae [78]   New England Aster

On moist prairies and meadows, along roads and streams statewide except
southeast lowlands. Blooms from August to October.
This is the tallest Aster growing in Missouri. To 8 feet (2.4 m) tall on a
leafy stalk that is branched above.
Flowerheads are quarter-sized, with many ray flowers in colors ranging
from crimson and magenta to shales of purple, with much variation in
color intensity.
Leaves are numerous, narrow lance-shaped, clasping the stem, from 2″
to 4″ (5 to 10 cm) long, a light green color.
Selections of this species have long been used as a garden plant.
Aster, Latin, "star," the shape of the flower; *novae-angliae,* Latin, "from
New England."

Aster turbinellus [91]   Prairie Aster

In rocky, dry open woods, glades, in acid soil, absent from the northwest. Blooms from August to November.

A much branched plant to 3½ feet tall (about 1 m).

Flowerheads in panicles and in great masses, deep lavender or purple, about 1″ (25 mm) across.

Leaves to 4½″ (12 cm) long, elliptical, pointed at both ends, without stems.

Steyermark considers *A. turbinellus* to have outstanding potential for cultivation.

Aster, Latin, "star;" *turbinellus*, Latin, "top-shaped," referring to the somewhat cylindrical involucre (the bracts).

250

Aster pilosis [27]   White Heath Aster

In old fields, gravel bars, waste places, statewide. Blooms from August to November.

Branched plant to nearly 5 feet (1.5 m) tall, branches either spreading or ascending, either hairy or not.

Flowerheads along the upper side of branches are about ¾″ (20 mm) across with up to 25 white or pale purplish ray florets. Very floriferous.

Leaves narrow, lance-shaped, without stems, alternate, from 1″ to 3″ (25 to 80 mm) long.

Aster, Latin, "star;" *pilosus*, Latin, "with soft hair."

Bidens polylepsis [51]   Beggar-ticks, Tickseed Sunflower

In wet prairies, waste places, along rivers, sloughs, ditches, roads and railroads statewide. Blooms from August to October.

There are 11 species of *Bidens* found in Missouri but only *B. polylepsis* has a wide distribution.

Much branched plants to 7 feet (2.1 m) tall, often dominating the landscape in moist situations in the fall.

Many flowerheads with bright yellow ray flowers, normally 8, which are pointed. The involucre—the bracts around the flowerhead—is conspicuous.

Leaves are compound with 3 to 5 divisions. The leaflets are narrow, sharply pointed, toothed.

The seeds look somewhat like ticks and have 2 pointed needle-like awns which attach themselves to Man and beast—thus "beggar's ticks."

Bidens, Latin, "two-toothed," describing the seeds; *polylepis*, Greek, "with many scales."

Chrysanthemum leucanthemum [22]   Ox-eye Daisy

In fields, meadows, roadsides, statewide. Blooms from May to August. Native of Europe.

An immigrant which provides beautiful displays in meadows and waste places. A plant with few branches, to 3 feet (90 cm) tall.

The flowerheads are large, to 2″ (50 mm) across, with white ray flowers and a yellow disk.

Leaves are of two kinds. Basal leaves on petioles are spoon-shaped and lobed, while alternate leaves along the stem are without stalks, narrow, with widely spaced teeth or lobes.

Chrysanthemum, Greek, means "golden flower" and refers to the type species of the Chrysanthemums, *C. coronarium*, which has lemon yellow flowerheads; *leucanthemum*, Greek, means "white flower" and describes our local species.

251

Chrysopsis villosa [47]   Golden Aster

In prairies, fields, along roads and railroads south of the Missouri River. Blooms from June to October.

A much-branched plant to 3 feet (90 cm) tall, one of two plants called Golden Aster in Missouri. In a few spots the Golden Aster covers entire valleys.

Bright yellow, aster-like flowers are produced profusely, the flowerheads about 1½″ (40 mm) across.

Leaves and stems are covered with soft hair. Leaves are alternate, stemless, sparsely toothed, to 3″ (75 mm) long, elliptical and pointed.

Chrysopsis is easily grown from seed.

Chrysopsis, Greek, means "golden eye;" *villosa*, Latin, "soft hairy."

Coreopsis lanceolata [35]   Tickseed Coreopsis

In rocky prairies, glades, along roads and railroads, in the Ozark region north to St. Louis County. Blooms from April to July.

Plants, to 2 feet (60 cm) high, are often found in profusion on glades.

Flowerheads on long stalks are golden yellow with ray flowers which have blunted, much-toothed tips. Sometimes these ray flowers form tubes. The flat disk also is yellow.

Leaves are very narrow, opposite, and restricted to the lower part of the plant.

The *Coreopsis* of the garden demands, like its wild relative, perfect drainage and poor soil.

Coreopsis, Greek, means "looking like a little bug," a reference to the shape of the seeds; *lanceolata,* Latin, "lance-shaped," refers to the leaves.

Coreopsis tripteris [47]   Tall Tickseed

In prairies, open woods, roadsides, statewide except southeast lowlands. Blooms from July to September.

A tall, late-blooming *Coreopsis,* to 8 feet (2.4 m) high, well branched on upper parts.

Flowerheads with 6 to 10 yellow ray flowers and a brown disk are to 1½" (40 mm) across and have an anise scent.

Leaves have stems and are distinctly 3 or 5 divided into leaflets or segments which are lance-shaped and without teeth.

Coreopsis, Greek, "looking like a little bug;" *tripteris,* Latin, "3-winged."

Coreopsis palmata   Stiff Tickseed

In prairies, fallow fields, roadsides, statewide. Blooms from May to July.

A rigid perennial to 3 feet (90 cm) tall.

The flowerhead is typical *Coreopsis* with the 3-toothed broad rays.

The leaves are 3-divided, narrow, much like the footprint of a crow or heron, sessile, opposite.

Coreopsis pubescens   Star Tickseed

In moist places, valleys, woods, on gravel beds in the Ozark region. Blooms from May to September.

Plants 2 to 4 feet (60 cm to 1.2 m) tall, usually not much branched.

Flowerheads with star-like, long bracts and from 8 to 10 much-toothed rays.

Lower leaves on short petioles, obovate, sometimes with small side lobes at the base. Many leaves on stems, stalkless, lance-shaped.

Echinacea pallida [66]   Pale-purple Coneflower

On limestone glades, prairies, along roads and railroads statewide except southeast lowlands. Blooms from May to July.

Usually unbranched plant to 3 feet (90 cm) tall, stems with spreading hair.

Flowerhead terminally on stalk. Ray flowers slender, strap-like with notched ends, hanging downward. Disk is knob-like, pointing upward, with yellow protruding stamens. Color of ray flowers is variable—rose, purple, magenta, or very rarely white.

Leaves very long and narrow, dotted with stiff hair.

Echinacea, Greek, the name of the hedgehog, a small European mammal

COREOPSIS

LANCEOLATA

PALMATA

TRIPTERIS

PUBESCENS

ERIGERON

PULCHELLUS

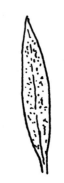

STRIGOSUS

ANNUUS

PHILADELPHICUS

254

with fierce spines; *pallida,* Latin, "pale."

Echinacea purpurea   Purple Coneflower

In openings in moist woods, wooded bottomland, prairies, scattered through mid-Missouri and eastern counties. Blooms from May to October.

One of our showiest wildflowers, to 3 feet (90 cm) tall.

Flowerheads carried terminally, with a madder-purple disk and up to 20 large bright or dark magenta rays which droop slightly, to 5″ (13 cm) across. Lower leaves rough above, egg-shaped, coarsely toothed, on petioles; the upper leaves with short or without stalks, lance-shaped, toothed.

255

Erigeron philadelphicus [8]   Philadelphia Fleabane

In fields, valleys, waste ground, along railroads, scattered throughout the state. Blooms from April to June.

Perennial plants to 3 feet (90 cm) high, branched toward the top, commonly soft hairy.

Flowerheads are small "Daisies" with 150 to 200 very narrow ray florets, carried terminally. No other *Erigeron* has that many ray florets, which are usually white but sometimes pink-lavender.

Lower leaves are spade-shaped (spatulate) with obtuse tips and short petioles. Upper leaves without stems, partially clasping.

Erigeron, Greek, *ery,* "early," and *geron,* "old man," thus, "old man in spring," referring to the massed silky parachutes of the seeds or the hoary appearance of young plants.

The genus *Erigeron* may well be the most populous of all plants in late spring.

| **Other Fleabanes with Daisy-like flowers:** |

Erigeron pulchellus   Robin's Plantain

In woods, clearings, along streams, missing from northwest counties. Blooms from April to June.

To 2 feet (60 cm) tall.

Few, quite large flowerheads with 50 to 75 longish rays.

Leaves very hairy, spoon-shaped at the base, narrower on stems.

Erigeron annuus   Daisy Fleabane, Whitetop Fleabane

In fields, prairies, waste places, statewide. Blooms from May to October.

Lower leaves on stalks, oblong, with teeth; upper leaves sessile, lanceolate. All leaves have conspicuous bristly hair on margins.

Erigeron strigosus Daisy Fleabane

In dry woods, fields, glades, statewide. Blooms from May to September.
Much like *E. annuus* but upper leaves very narrow, linear.

> **Fleabanes with very small flowers:**

Erigeron canadensis Horse Weed

In fields, prairies, waste places, statewide. Blooms from June to November. (Note late flowering.)
Very tall, commonly to 7 feet (2.1 m), single stalks with many leaves and dense, terminal inflorescence.
Many tiny flowerheads, only ³⁄₁₆″ (5 mm) wide. Rays are so small they are practically invisible.
Leaves are many, long, lanceolate. Stems and leaves hairy.

Erigeron divaricatus Dwarf Fleabane

In fields, prairies, waste places, statewide. Blooms from May to September.
A low, much branched plant, extremely hairy, to 12″ (30 cm) tall.
Flowerheads insignificant.
Leaves linear, only 1″ (25 mm) long. Note bushy, ash-grey appearance.

Helenium amarum [46] *(tenuifolium)* Fine-leaved Sneeze-weed, Bitterweed, Yellow Dog Fennel

In fields, waste places, along roads and railroads in southern and west-central Missouri. Blooms from June to November.
A much branched low plant, normally to 12″ (30 cm) high, but sometimes to 2 feet.
Flowerheads yellow, the ray flowers drooping and notched, the disk pointing skyward, bowl-shaped.
Leaves linear or threadlike, only to 1½″ (4 cm) long, in great profusion along the stems, with smaller leaves arising from the axils of larger ones.
The plant contains a poison which causes milk to taste bitter, thus Bitterweed.
Helenium, there is no record if the scientist who named the plant had

Helenus or Helena in mind; *amarum,* Latin, "bitter." The powdered disk flowers, used as snuff, cause violent and long continued sneezing, therefore Sneezeweed.

Helenium autumnale [51]   Sneezeweed

In moist areas in meadows, ditches, prairies, along streams, scattered statewide except in southeast lowlands. Blooms from August to November.
A late blooming Sneezeweed, to 6 feet (1.8 m) tall, branching toward the top. Stems conspicuously winged.
Flowerheads yellow with from 10 to 18 ray flowers with notched ends which are reflexed. The large disk protrudes dome-like.
Leaves are alternate, narrow lance-shaped, with or without a few teeth, stalkless.
All parts of the plant contain a bitter substance which may be poisonous.
Helenium, for Helena or Helenus; *autumnale,* Latin, "occurring in the fall."

257

Helenium flexuosum   Purple-headed Sneezeweed

This species is called *H. nudiflorum* by several authors.
In moist places, bottomlands, ditches, roadsides, south of the Missouri River and in east-central counties. Blooms from June to November.
To 3 feet tall (.9 m), branched toward the top.
Flowerhead with deep brown-purple, domed disk and 10 to 15 drooping yellow rays; the only Helenium with a dark brown center.
Leaves lance-shaped, the lower ones tapering into winged stalks, with or without a few fine teeth.

Helianthus tuberosus [49]   Jerusalem Artichoke

In wet areas on prairies, waste ground, along roads, in moist or dry open woods, absent from the Ozark region. Blooms from August to October.
Very tall, to at least 12 feet (3.6 m), much branched, very hairy stalk.
The flowerheads, Sunflower yellow, have 12 to 20 ray flowers and are up to 3″ (75 mm) across, often with a chocolate-like scent.
Leaves are thick, lance-shaped, coarsely toothed, rough hairy above and downy below, to 9″ (23 cm) long, prominently 3-veined.
Roots produce edible, potato-like tubers in irregular shapes which were eaten by the Indians. The plant is cultivated for food in many parts of the world. The tubers can be served to diabetics.
The name Jerusalem Artichoke is believed to be based on a misunderstanding of the French word "Girasol."
Helianthus, Greek, "sun-flower," because the flowerheads turn with the sun each day; *tuberosus,* Latin, "with tubers."

Helianthus mollis   Hairy Sunflower

On prairies, roadsides, fields, absent from northwest Missouri. Blooms
from July to October.

Plants to 4 feet (1.2 m) tall.

Flowerheads all yellow with 15 to 25 rays.

Leaves rough on both sides, lanceolate, toothed, on short stalks. Leaf
tissue joins with leaf stalk (decurrent).

Helianthus grosseserratus [49]   Sawtooth Sunflower

In prairies, moist fields and meadows, along roadsides and railroads, statewide except southeast lowlands. Blooms from July to October.

258

A giant to 16 feet (4.8 m) tall, usually branched. This and other Sunflower
species hybridize readily, making identification difficult. There are at
least 11 known hybrids of *H. grosseserratus* alone.

Flowerheads are typical Sunflowers, to 3½″ (9 cm) across, with from 10
to 20 rather broad ray flowers.

Leaves alternate, narrow lance-shaped, about 2½″ (65 mm) wide and 10″
(25 cm) long, toothed.

Helianthus, Greek, "sun-flower," because the flowerheads turn to follow
the sun; *grosseserratus*, Latin, "coarsely toothed" or "saw-like."

**Four additional species, of the 15 Helianthus in Missouri, have wide dis-
tribution.**

Helianthus annuus   Common Sunflower

In waste and cultivated areas, roadsides, scattered statewide. Blooms from
July to November.

Extremely variable in height and appearance. This is the ancestor of the
cultivated plants with huge flowerheads, which will revert to the
original size in slow stages. Stems and leaves rough.

Disk dark brown or purple, rays yellow. Flowerheads often with many
ray flowers.

Leaves alternate, though those lowest on the stem may be opposite, spade-
shaped, more or less toothed.

Helianthus hirsutus   Stiff-haired Sunflower

In dry open woods, prairies, roadsides, statewide. Blooms from July to
October. To 4 feet (1.2 m) tall.

Only 8 to 15 rays, disk and rays yellow.

Leaves without teeth, densely hairy, on short stalks, lanceolate with
rounded base. Stems also hairy.

HELIANTHUS

HIRSUTUS

TUBEROSUS

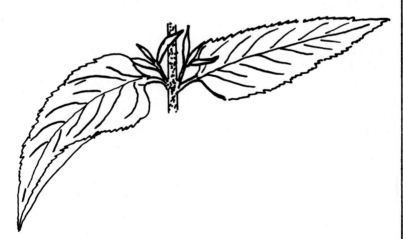

HELIANTHUS

ANNUUS

GROSSESERRATUS

LAETIFLORUS   MOLLIS

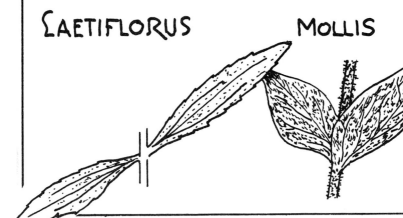

Helianthus laetiflorus   Prairie Sunflower

On prairies of northern and western Missouri. Blooms from August to
October. A tall Sunflower, to 7 feet (2.1 m).
Flowerheads all yellow with 12 to 25 rays.
Leaves rough on both sides, lanceolate, toothed, on short stalks. Leaf
tissue joins with leaf stalk (decurrent).

Parthenium integrifolium [18]   American Feverfew, Wild Quinine, Prairie Dock

On prairies, glades, rocky woods, statewide except southeast lowlands and
northwest counties. Blooms from May to September.
Perennial to 3 feet (90 cm) tall.
Small, whitish flowerheads in branching terminal inflorescences.
Leaves with long, slightly winged stems on lower part of stalk, becoming
stemless higher up, are paddle-shaped, coarsely and irregularly toothed,
generally without hair.
The names Feverfew and Wild Quinine indicate that the plant was used
medicinally.
Parthenium, Greek, from *parthenos*, "virgin," a reference to the fact that
only the ray flowers are fertile; *integrifolium*, Latin, "entire-leaved."

261

Parthenium hispidum   Hairy Feverfew

On limestone glades and prairies in the Ozarks. Blooms from May to
October.
Very similar to *P. integrifolium* but the entire plant is hairy.
Hispidum, Latin, "hairy."

Polymnia canadensis [24]   Leaf-cup or Small Flower Leaf-cup

On loose limestone rubble and slopes of the Ozark region. Blooms from
May to October.
Tall, straight-growing, somewhat weedy, sticky-hairy, from 3 to 5 feet
(.9 to 1.5 m) tall.
Flowerheads few, in terminal clusters, each only ¼″ (13 mm) across. Ray
flowers no more than 5, white, sometimes missing. These have pistils
and are fertile. The disk flowers are "perfect," that is they have both
male and female floral parts, but are sterile. Prominent bracts around
the flowerheads.
Leaves are pinnately 3 to 5 lobed, to 10″ (25 cm) long, the lobes with
teeth. The leafblade does not extend to the leafstalk (petiole) in this
species.
Polymnia, Greek, is named for the Muse Polyhymnia.

Polymnia uvedalia   Yellow-flower Leaf-cup

In low woods and at the base of bluffs in southern and southeastern Missouri. Blooms from July to September.

It has 10 to 15 yellow disk flowers, larger than *P. canadensis.*

Leaves are broad, palmately lobed, the leaf tissue extending into the leaf-stalk.

Ratibida pinnata [44]   Gray-head Coneflower

On prairies, along roads and railroads, borders of woods, statewide except southeast lowlands. Blooms from late May to September.

262   Single or branched stalk to over 3 feet (90 cm) tall. Entire plant rough-hairy.

Flowerheads with a few (3-7) drooping, yellow ray flowers which can be to 3″ (75 mm) long, while the grayish disk rises cone-like above the petticoat of ray flowers.

Leaves pinnately divided into 3 to 7 segments which are toothed and narrowly lance-shaped.

The name *Ratibida* has no explanation; *pinnata*, Latin, refers to the pinnate leaves.

Rudbeckia hirta [42]   Black-eyed Susan

In open woods, fields, waste ground, along roads and railroads statewide. Blooms from May to October.

To 2½ feet (76 cm) tall, usually unbranched, very hairy.

Normally one flowerhead on a stalk. The ray flowers are yellow or orange-yellow, from 10 to 20, with a flowerhead from 2″ to 4″ (5 to 10 cm) across. The disk is egg-shaped, never "black-eyed" but deep brown or purple-brown.

Leaves hairy, without stems, though basal leaves with stems are found, thick, either toothed or not, lanceolate.

The species is so variable and has such a wide distribution that botanists have proposed that it be divided into a number of species.

Rudbeckia, named after two professors Rudbeck, father and son, 1630-1702 and 1660-1740, one a teacher of Linnaeus at Upsala; *hirta*, Latin, "hairy."

Rudbeckia missouriensis   Missouri Black-eyed Susan

Mainly on limestone glades, a plant of hot, dry, rocky places in the Ozarks. Blooms from late June to October.

About 18″ (45 cm) tall, conspicuously hairy.

Much like *R. hirta* in the appearance of the flowerheads.

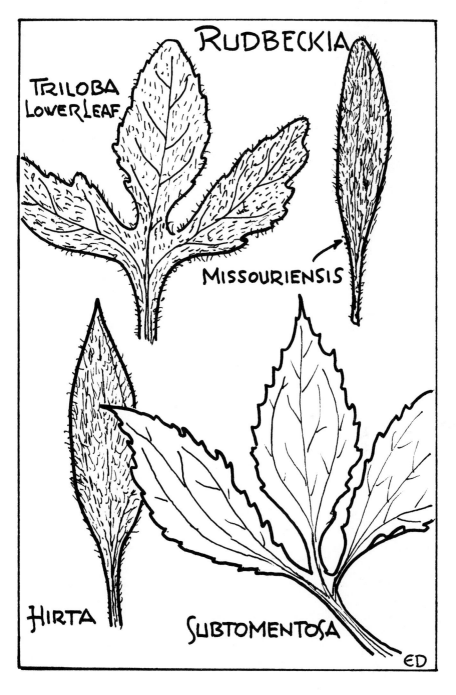

RUDBECKIA

TRILOBA
LOWER LEAF

MISSOURIENSIS

263

HIRTA

SUBTOMENTOSA

ED

RUDBECKIA LACINIATA

Upper leaves linear, basal leaves either linear or lance-shaped.

Rudbeckia triloba [44] Brown-eyed Susan, Thin-leaved Coneflower

In low wet woods, along streams, at the base of bluffs, statewide except southeast lowlands. Blooms from June to November.
Branching stem to 5 feet (1.5 m) tall.
Flowerheads smaller than *R. hirta*, with from 8 to 12 bright yellow or orange-yellow ray flowers. The disk is deep purple-brown. Flowers numerous and nearly 2″ (50 mm) across.
Only the lower leaves are 3-lobed, the middle lobe being larger and longer. Upper leaves with or without stems, thin, often with coarse teeth, narrow lance-shaped. Both types usually hairy.
Rudbeckia, named for two professors Rudbeck; *triloba,* Latin, "three-lobed," referring to the lower leaves.

Rudbeckia subtomentosa Sweet Coneflower

In moist places near streams or in prairies, roadsides, scattered statewide. Blooms from July to October.
Tall, to 6 feet (1.8 m), but usually lower, very hairy, branched.
The flowerheads have a brown or purple-brown disk which is nearly half-domed. Rays yellow, 12 to 20.
Leaves near base often 3-lobed, the higher ones often oblong lanceolate, both types with coarse teeth.

Rudbeckia laciniata Wild Goldenglow, Tall Coneflower

In valleys near streams or other low, moist habitat, statewide except southeast. Blooms from July to September.
This rank-growing dweller of the floodplains can reach 9 feet (2.7 m).
The flowerhead differs from the other *Rudbeckias* in having a greenish-yellow disk and only from 6 to 10 bright yellow rays.
Lower leaves are long-petioled, very large, pinnately 3 to 7 divided, the segments showing a variety of toothed or lobed appearances. Upper leaves are much smaller, often 3-lobed, with or without teeth.

Senecio obovatus [34] Squaw-weed, Round-leaved Groundsel

In rich and rocky woods, on slopes, at bases of bluffs, generally south of the Missouri River. Blooms from early April to June.
A perennial to 2 feet (60 cm) tall, generally growing in groups.
Flowerheads about the size of a quarter, somewhat ragged, both ray and disk flowers rich yellow.

Leaves mostly basal, rounded to spoon-shaped with rounded teeth, the leaf blade conspicuously continued into the petiole, to 3½″ (9 cm) long. Few small, sessile leaves on the stem.

Senecio, Latin, "old man," because of the white fuzz of the seeds; *obovatus*, Latin, "oblong ovate."

Senecio aureus   Golden Ragwort

On low, moist ground, near springs, generally south of the Missouri River. Blooms from April to June.

Flowers are the same as S. *obovatus*, with a delicate scent.

Basal leaves are heart-shaped, on long petioles, with rounded teeth.

266

Senecio plattensis   Prairie Ragwort

In prairies, dry upland places, scattered statewide. Blooms in May and June.

Plants to 18″ (45 cm) tall.

Flowers have fewer rays than S. *obovatus*.

Basal leaves on very long petioles, spoon-shaped, very hairy, with many rounded teeth.

Senecio glabellus   Butterweed

In the floodplains of the Mississippi and Missouri Rivers and in the southeast. Blooms from April to June.

An impressive branched plant to 3 feet (90 cm) tall.

Flowerheads abundant, with rich golden yellow flowers.

Leaves pinnate (like a feather) along stems; no basal leaves.

Silphium perfoliatum [48]   Cup Plant, Cup Rosin Weed, Indian Cup, Carpenter's Weed

In meadows, low ground near streams and ponds, waste places, statewide except southeast lowlands. Blooms from July to September.

Under favorable conditions grows to 8 feet (2.4 m) tall.

Flowerheads are numerous, with 20 to 30 slender yellow rays.

Opposite leaves on upper part of the plant are joined around the stem forming a cup which holds water. Leaves are huge, to 12″ (30 cm) long, with wavy margins, rough on both sides, oval shape, pointed and covered with dots.

Rosin Weed is a name given to several *Silphiums* because they contain a sticky rosin. The name Carpenter's Weed comes from the square stem.

Silphium, Greek, the name of an African plant; *perfoliatum*, Latin for "surrounding the stem."

SENECIO

AUREUS

BASAL LEAF

PLATTENSIS

BASAL LEAF

GLABELLUS

STEM LEAF

OBOVATUS

BASAL LEAF

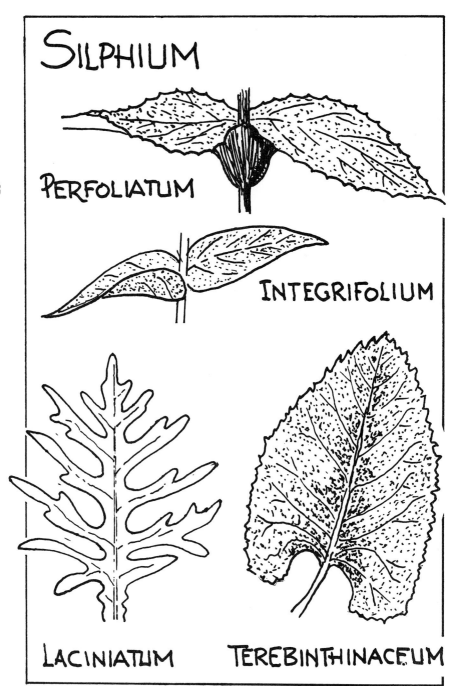

SILPHIUM

PERFOLIATUM

INTEGRIFOLIUM

LACINIATUM

TEREBINTHINACEUM

Silphium terebinthinaceum [48] Prairie Dock

On glades, prairies, usually on limestone, in the Ozark region and central
and northeastern counties. Blooms from July to October.
Basal leaves, heart-shaped, dark green, upright on long stalks, to 12″
(30 cm) long and 8″ (20 cm) wide. These huge and crowded leaves
develop in spring and early summer.
A usually naked flower stalk, to nearly 10 feet (3 m) tall, develops later,
branched toward the top, and carries the yellow flowerheads. These
have from 8 to 20 yellow ray flowers at the end of long side branches.
Both the basal leaves and the unusually long stalk with the daisy-like
flowers create much curiosity.
Silphium, Greek, the name of another plant, transferred arbitrarily by
Linnaeus to this genus; *terebinthinaceum*, Greek, means "containing
turpentine," for the rosin which gives this species a distinct and agree-
able scent.

269

Silphium integrifolium Rosin Weed

In prairies, fields, roadsides, borders of woods statewide. Blooms from
July to September.
A tall plant to 7 feet (2.1 m). Stems without hair or very minor hairiness.
Numerous yellow flowerheads.
Leaves mostly opposite, rough, stalkless—but not surrounding the stalk—
ovate-lanceolate, with a few teeth or none.
The plant contains a resinous sap.

Silphium laciniatum Compass Plant

In prairies, glades, roadsides, absent from southeast Missouri. Blooms from
July to September.
To 8 feet (nearly 2.5 m) tall and showy, rough hairy and resinous.
Yellow flowerheads along the long stalk.
Leaves deeply cleft almost to mid-rib with irregular, pointed lobes. The
lower leaves have their edges turned north and south when growing
in full sun.
A gummy substance, which the Indians used as chewing gum, appears
on the upper stems.

Solidago juncea [47] Early Goldenrod

In prairies, dry, open rocky woods, usually on acid soils, in the Ozark
region north to St. Louis County. Blooms from June to October.
This Goldenrod was chosen to represent a type. There are 25 species of
Goldenrod in Missouri, usually single-stemmed with a yellow inflores-

cence. *S. juncea* is the earliest flowering species.

Stout stalks to 4 feet (1.2 m) tall, branching toward the top into curved flower-bearing branchlets.

The yellow flowerheads contain both ray and disk florets which are fertilized by insects. Flowerheads are carried on the upper side of the flowering stems only and point upward.

Leaves are willow-like, narrow with variable toothing, the teeth either closely or widely spaced, Lower leaves can be to 12″ (30 cm) long and are lance-shaped, but leaves become shorter the higher they grow on the stalk.

Goldenrod is falsely accused of causing hayfever, an affliction caused by wind-borne pollen, while Goldenrod depends on insects for fertilization.

Solidago, meaning unknown; *juncea,* Latin, "rush-like."

Solidago speciosa [50]   Goldenrod

In prairies, meadows, dry, rocky open woods, scattered statewide except in the Ozark region. Blooms from August to November.

A handsome plant, unbranched, to 3 feet (90 cm) or more high.

Flowers possibly the showiest of the 25 Goldenrods found in Missouri. The flowerheads are arranged spirally and terminally around the stalk, in contrast to the one-sided inflorescence of other Goldenrods, forming a plume-like panicle. Flowerheads are yellow and rather large.

Leaves are alternate, lanceolate, long-pointed, with stipules.

Solidago, meaning unknown; *speciosa,* Latin, "showy" or "good looking."

Verbesina virginica [27]   White Crown-beard, Wing-stem, Frostweed

In rocky open woods, along streams, in valleys, in southern Missouri. Blooms from August to October.

A perennial plant with a winged stalk to 7 feet (2.1 m) tall. The wings are extensions of leaf tissue along the stem.

Flowerheads small, 1″ to 1½″ (25 to 40 mm) across with only a few, usually 3 to 5, white ray flowers. Flowerheads are clustered terminally.

Leaves alternate, ovately lance-shaped, with widely spaced teeth.

This is one of the few plants which produce "frost flowers" when water is forced through cracks just above the root system during the first severe freeze of the season, forming contorted ice shapes.

Verbesina, the meaning of the name is unknown.

Verbesina helianthoides [43]   Crown-beard, Wing-stem

In rocky, dry open woods, prairies, along roads and railroads, south of the

Missouri River and in east-central counties. Blooms from late May to October.

Straight stalk to 5 feet (1.5 m) tall with distinct wings, extensions of leaf tissue along the stem.

Few flowerheads with 8 to 15 yellow ray flowers which are spread horizontally, not drooping. These often vary in length on the same flowerhead.

Leaves broadly ovate, without stems, rough above, soft hairy below. The lower leaves are opposite, those higher up alternate, all with widely spaced small teeth.

Verbesina, the meaning of the name is not known; *helianthoides*, Greek, "like a Sunflower."

271

Verbesina alternifolia   Yellow Ironweed

In moist woods, valleys, near streams, statewide. Blooms from August to October.

This plant is also known as *Actinomeris alternifolia*.

Similar to *V. helianthoides* but the many yellow flowerheads have only from 2 to 8 drooping rays and the leaves are all alternate with the leaf tissue extending along the stalks.

Leaf shape is lanceolate with fine teeth.

Ambrosia trifida [56]   Ragweed, Giant or Great Ragweed, Horse Weed, Buffalo Weed

The genus *Ambrosia* does not fit into the 3 subdivisions of the Composite Family—ray flowers only, disk flowers only, both ray and disk flowers —and was, until recently, a separate family, *Ambrosiaceae*.

In rich soil in waste places, fields, along roads, statewide. Blooms from July to September.

Annual, much branched, to 6 feet (1.8 m) tall and sometimes more. Frequently growing by the thousands in bottomlands.

Male flowers (pollen bearing) are quite small, greenish, in loose, terminal, slender racemes. Female flowers are nearly hidden in leaf axils.

Leaves very large, soft, broad, usually 3 or 5-lobed, but also unlobed, toothed. The lobes have sharp points.

The pollen of this plant is the major source of hayfever as it is carried by air currents.

The seeds are an important food for quail, doves, prairie chickens, ducks, pheasants, turkeys, and even raccoons. Deer browse the leaves. Prehistoric Indians cultivated Ragweed for the seeds which were larger in the cultivated plants than those of our wild plants.

Ambrosia, Greek and Latin, the name of several plants, meaning "the food of the gods;" *trifida*, Latin, "three-lobed," referring to the leaves.

Ambrosia artemisiifolia   Common Ragweed

In fields, waste places, roadsides, statewide. Blooms from July to November.

To around 2½ feet (75 cm) tall.

While the floral arrangement resembles that of the above species, the leaves are totally different—ornamental, deeply dissected, feather-like, with scallopped margins.

This hairy plant is a major contributor to "hay fever" through its wind-carried pollen. When crushed, all parts of the plant have a strong odor which is disagreeable to many.

Index to the FAMILIES represented by the species described in the text

A) BOTANICAL ORDER

273

B) FAMILIES IN COMMON NAME ORDER

°superseded Family names

*superseded Family names

INDEX OF GENERA AND SPECIES

Common and Botanical Names

See separate Index for Families, pages 273-274

275

276

277

278

279

280

281

283

284

285

FIELD NOTES

FIELD NOTES

FIELD NOTES

FIELD NOTES

FIELD NOTES

FIELD NOTES